The Year of Blood

Some Books from Social Science Press and Aurum Books

Shades of Difference: Selected Writings of Rabindranath Tagore wth Audio Visual Material, *Tagore and His World* (HB)
Edited by RADHA CHAKRAVARTY

Calcutta: The Stormy Decades (HB)
Edited by TANIKA SARKAR AND SEKHAR BANDYOPADHYAY

Dalit Women: Honour and Patriarchy in South India (HB)
CLARINDA STILL

Tamil Brahmans: The Creation of a Middle-Class Caste (HB)
CJ FULLER AND HARIPRIYA NARASIMHAN

Persistence of Poverty in India (HB)
Edited by NANDINI GOOPTU AND JONATHAN PARRY

Savage Attack: Tribal Insurgency in India (HB)
Edited by CRISPIN BATES AND ALPA SHAH

The Year of Blood: Essays on the Revolt of 1857 (HB)
RUDRANGSHU MUKHERJEE

The Autobiography of a Revolutionary in British India (HB)
KALI GHOSH

4 Victoria Terrace: Memoirs of a Surgeon (HB)
SUBIR K. CHATTERJEE

The Many Worlds of Sarala Devi: A Diary
Translated by SUKHENDU RAY and
The Tagores and Sartorial Styles: A Photo Essay (HB)
MALAVIKA KARLEKAR

Viramma: Life of a Dalit (PB)
VIRAMMA, JOSIANE RACINE, AND JEAN-LUC RACINE

Everyday Nationalism: Women of the Hindu Right (HB)
KALYANI DEVAKI MENON

Marriage, Love, Caste & Kinship Support (HB)
Lived Experiences of the Urban Poor in India
SHALINI GROVER

Religious Division and Social Conflict: The Emergence of Hindu Nationalism in Rural India (PB)
PEGGY FROERER

Literature and Nationalist Ideology: Writing Histories of Indian Languages(PB)
HANS HARDER

The Everyday State and Society in Modern India (PB)
Edited by CJ FULLER AND VERONIQUE BENEI

Economics and Its Stories (HB)
AMAL SANYAL

Telecommunications Industry in India: State Business and Labour in a Global Economy(HB)
DILIP SUBRAMANIAM

Cultural History of Modern India (PB)
Edited by MEENAKSHI KHANNA

Delhi: Ancient History (PB)
Edited by UPINDER SINGH

Income Poverty and Beyond
Human Development in India
Edited by RAJA J CHELLIAH AND R SUDERSHAN

The Politics of the Pharmaceutical Industry and Access to Medicines: World Pharmacy and India (HB)
Edited by HANS LOGREN

SERIES: EVERYDAY LIFE OF POLITICAL STRUGGLES

Windows into a Revolution: Ethnographies of Maoism in India and Nepal (HB)
Edited by ALPA SHAH AND JUDITH PETTIGREW

Rebels from the Mud Houses: Dalits and the Making of the Maoist Revolution in Bihar (HB)
GEORGE KUNNATH

Unruly Hills: Nature and Nation in India's North-East (HB)
BENGT G. KARLSSON

SERIES: GERMAN WRITINGS ON INDIA AND SOUTH ASIA

'When the war began we heard of several kings': South Asian Prisoners in World War I Germany (HB)
Edited by FRANSIZKA ROY, HEIKE LIEBAU AND RAVI AHUJA

Cultural Encounters in India
The Local Co-Workers of the Tranquebar Mission, 18th-19th centuries (HB)
HEIKE LIEBAU

'Everwhere is Becoming the Same'? Regulating IT-work between India and Germany (HB)
NICOLE MAYER-AHUJA

SERIES: FRENCH WRITINGS ON INDIA AND SOUTH ASIA

Scholars and Prophets: Sociology of India from France in the 19th and 20th Centuries (HB)
ROLAND LARDINOIS

Tocqueville in India (HB)
JEAN ALPHONSE BERNARD

AURUM BOOKS

Sabotage (PB)
ANITA AGNIHOTRI
Translated by ARUNAVA SINHA

Opium Poppy (PB)
HUBERT HADDAD
Translated by RENUKA GEORGE

Forthcoming SSP

Much Ado Over Coffee: The Social History of the Indian Coffee House (HB)
BHASWATI BHATTACHARYA

Forthcoming Aurum Books

Revolutionary Passions (HB)
HAMIT BOZARSLAN, GILLES BATAILLON AND CHRISTOPHE JAFFRELOT
Translated by SOMA DATTA GUPTA

Gandhi: Anti-Biography of a Great Soul (HB)
MICHAËL DE SAINT-CHERON
Translated by ASHA N. SPAAK

The Year of Blood

Essays on the Revolt of 1857

By

Rudrangshu Mukherjee

SOCIAL
SCIENCE
PRESS

Published by
Esha Béteille
Social Science Press
69 Jor Bagh, New Delhi 110 003

First published in 2014
Paperback Edition in 2016

Mangal Pandey: Brave Martyr or Accidental Hero?
First published by Penguin Books 2007

Distributed by
Orient Blackswan Pvt. Ltd.
Bangalore Bhopal Bhubaneshwar Chandigarh
Chennai Ernakulam Guwahati Hyderabad Jaipur
Kolkata Lucknow Mumbai New Delhi Noida Patna
www.orientblackswan.com

ISBN: 978-93-83166-13-8

Set in Plantin 10/12.1
Typeset by Eleven Arts, Delhi 110 035
Printed by Sumit Advertising,
2, DLF (part) Industrial Area, Moti Nagar,
New Delhi-110 015

To three British friends who love India
Anabel Loyd, Simon Parkes and of course Toby Sinclair

The Enfield Rifle

Courtesy: *http://indianhistoryforu.blogspot.in/2012/05/revolt-of-1857-ad.html*

Contents

Illustrations

Introduction: In Pursuit of a Revolt

This volume brings together my occasional essays on 1857 and a small book that was, in terms of its length no more than a longish essay. The essays are chronologically arranged. My fascination with the revolt of 1857 dates back to my undergraduate days in Presidency College in Calcutta and my dissatisfaction with that hoary old chestnut that appeared all too frequently in school-leaving and undergraduate question papers about what to call the rebellion—mutiny, war of independence, feudal uprising, what have you. The dissatisfaction and the quest for alternative ways to look at the revolt were whetted when our professor, Hiren Chakrabarti, somewhat out of the blue, asked me to write a comment on the Azamgarh Proclamation that had been issued by a rebel prince in the summer of 1857. I remember that he dictated the entire document to me from Ainslee Embree's collection of writings and documents on 1857.[1] That document drew me and my tutorial essay outgrew itself by many words and pages.

I showed that essay to Barun De and Sumit Sarkar who encouraged me with their detailed comments to develop the essay, and the former directed me to read the essays of Eric Stokes, which had started coming out in journals from the late 1960s. All this was of course far beyond an undergraduate's call of duty but precocious, as I was, I pursued in developing what had begun life as a tutorial essay. It was eventually published while I was still a student. It is

[1]Ainslee Embree, *1857 in India: Mutiny or War of Independence?* (Boston, 1963).

included in this volume as much as an example of a youthful folly as also a signpost for the beginning of a journey.

As a post graduate student in the Centre for Historical Studies in Jawaharlal Nehru University, I had no opportunity to pursue my interest on 1857. The revolt had no place in the courses taught there. Given the nature of the courses and the teaching in JNU, the natural path for a student eager to do research on a historical theme was to choose a subject related to Indian nationalism or modern Indian economic history. And many of my friends did do this. The revolt of 1857 refused to leave me, however. I decided I would work on some aspect of it for my doctoral dissertation and I recall one of my old teachers wondering if there was anything new to say on the uprising. I was convinced, after reading Stokes's essays that the most important questions regarding the revolt had not even been posed because of the obsession with nomenclature among historians who wrote on 1857.[2] Barun De's concurrence strengthened my conviction and he guided my first steps in research.

This was the background to my Oxford DPhil, which became my first book, *Awadh in Revolt.*[3] The task of finishing a thesis within the stipulated time offered by a scholarship and then turning a dissertation into a book precluded the writing of short essays. Between my first book and the writing of the second essay, an important intervention took place in the writing of modern Indian history. This was the publication in the early 1980s of the first three volumes of *Subaltern Studies* and of Ranajit Guha's *Elementary Aspects of Peasant Emergency in Colonial India.* These not only challenged the way modern India had been written about by historians but also offered fresh perspectives for the study of peasant and popular insurgency. These perspectives exerted a strong influence on my evolving understanding of the nature of popular insurgency and rebel violence in the uprising of 1857.

There were two obvious features of the revolt: one was violence and the other was power. The year 1857 saw acts of violence that were unprecedented and often incredible. The exhibition of violence on both the British and the rebel sides was an exhibition of power. The second essay on the massacres that the rebels carried out in Kanpur (or Cawnpore as the British preferred to call it) analyses how the killings were manifestations of rebel power. The essay was written

[2]Stokes tellingly called this obsession a 'mental cramp.'

[3]*Awadh in Revolt, 1857–58: A Study of Popular Resistance* (Delhi, 1984).

for a seminar in Princeton University. The response it had, and the encouragement I received from my colleagues there, especially from Lawrence Stone, made me write a book on what happened in Kanpur and how it was depicted.[4] A somewhat revised version of the essay forms a chapter in the book but what is reprinted here is as the essay was first published in the journal *Past and Present*.[5] The essay gave rise to a small controversy on the pages of the journal. The critique of my piece is by Barbara English. My reply to her is not included here, but I feel readers should know that my views did not go unchallenged. '

The essay, 'The Sepoy Mutinies Revisited', which appears in this book as 'The Sipahi and the Sepoy Mutinies' was written for a festschrift volume for Eric Stokes that Narayani Gupta and Mushirul Hasan put together. When they asked me to contribute an essay for the volume, I readily agreed not only because Stokes had influenced my work but also because he had examined my DPhil thesis, in spite of his serious illness. The essay drew on some of the insights offered by Ranajit Guha and pointed to the links between the mutinies of the sepoys that began the rebellion and uprisings of the civil population that invariably followed the mutinies across the North India.

Much to my surprise, there was at the beginning of this century a request to reprint my book on Awadh in paperback. I agreed with alacrity and wrote for the reprint an introduction by way of reflections on where the subject had gone since the book had been published in 1984.[6] One of the things that the introduction to the paperback edition tried to do was to trace the influence of *Elementary Aspects of Peasant Insurgency* on the analysis of 1857. The introduction is reprinted here because it does stand on its own as an independent essay. It also notes how my own ideas on the study of the revolt has developed and changed.

As a historian of 1857, I tried my best to stay away from the official celebrations that took place on the occasion of the uprising's 150th anniversary. Even though I escaped somewhat unscathed from the official series of seminars that took place, I could not resist the temptation of writing something to mark the anniversary

[4] *Spectre of Violence: The Massacres in Kanpur in the Revolt of 1857 in India* (Delhi, 1998).

[5] '"Satan Let Loose upon Earth": The Massacres in Kanpur in the Revolt of 1857 in India,' *Past and Present* (August 1991).

[6] It was reprinted by Permanent Black in 2002.

of an event whose historian I had chosen to become for good or for bad. I decided, at the invitation of the department of history of Delhi University, to look at two texts that had been produced in the centenary year of 1857. One was the history of the revolt that the government of India commissioned in 1957, S.N. Sen's *1857*, and the other was S.B. Chaudhuri's *Civil Rebellion in the Uprising of 1857–58*, a work that bore no stamp of governmental approval except for a Foreword from the then vice president of India, Sarvepalli Radhakrishnan. I tried to analyse in that essay some of the unresolved tensions and contradictions that were evident in the work of two eminent historians influenced by the spirit of Indian nationalism. This is the last essay in this book.

The next essay included in the book had an odd origin. Around 2004–05, there were reports in the press that the film director, Ketan Mehta, was making a film on Mangal Pandey with Amir Khan as the lead actor. I was curious but my curiosity was chanelled into a different direction when a friend from Penguin India called to ask if I would be interested in doing a biography of Mangal Pandey. My first response was in the negative and I explained to her that I was reasonably familiar with the material that existed about Mangal Pandey and I could not see this filling out a book. She was persuasive and the prospect of doing a biography from very thin material appeared to me to be an intellectual challenge. I wrote the book, which is by no means a biography in the conventional sense of the term. Also, the book turned out to be a slim volume since what I had written was no more than a long essay. The full text of the book (complete with appendix) is reprinted here.

Historic Kashmere Gate, Delhi

Bullet-ridden Kashmiri Gate

Courtesy: *Aditi Chandra (Private collection)*

This gate is now a familiar site for the inhabitants of Old Delhi. Many of those who pass by it are perhaps unaware that near this gate many important encounters took place between the rebels who were defending Delhi and the British troops who were trying to recover the city. It was in one such encounter that John Nicholson a British officer renowned for his avenging zeal fell fighting. As long as the rebels retained control over Delhi it was the seat of the makeshift administration that the rebel leaders were trying to establish. It was from Delhi in the name of the Mughal Emperor, Bahadur Shah, that some of the important ishtahars or proclamations were issued.

No. 898.—VOL. XXXII.] SATURDAY, JANUARY 16, 1858. [WITH A SUPPLEMENT, FIVEPENCE

INDIA.

THE situation of affairs in India has assumed a new character. It is no longer an insurrectionary movement in the Bengal army which we have to face—it is a war in Oude. The attraction which that province seems to possess for the mutineers would almost seem to indicate that within it lay the original seeds of the revolt. It is evidently in that territory that the first act of the re-assertion of our rule in the East is to be played out; and it is probable that it will also be the scene of the last. On the one hand, all the dispersed and routed sepoy bands make for Oude as their point of concentration, having, as is well known, a force of disciplined men amounting to 70,000 or 80,000, which formed the army of the late Sovereign of that kingdom, around which they can gather. On the other hand, all the preparations of the British Commander-in-Chief seem to point to a strategy which involves the overrunning of the province from different points, and pressing the whole force of the enemy into such a position as will place the issue of events on a great battle, probably before the capital city, from before which Sir Colin Campbell has recently retired, falling back on Cawnpore, which station will probably be the western pivot of movements hereafter. The order for the concentration of troops at Benares, under Colonel Franks, an officer of repute, and well known in India under the soubriquet of Tiger Franks, would seem to indicate a movement upwards, on the north bank of the Ganges, instead of the passage, as hitherto, of small bodies of troops by the south side to Allahabad. On the south-east the Ghoorka force, although said to have received a check from the rebels, would advance from Azimghur, while the Nepaulese contingent sent by Jung Bahadoor would come down from the north-east. Supposing such a scheme of a campaign to be in contemplation, it would appear to be founded on some such plan as that adopted in the great hunting expeditions of the country, in which the game is driven in from every quarter to the centre of a circle, there to be dealt with after the manner of hunters towards beasts of prey. There is no fault to be found with such a conception; the only question is, has the Commander-in-Chief the means at his disposal for carrying it into execution? In the imperfect state of the information which has reached this country it is not possible to come to any decided opinion on that head. We know that long ere this the whole of the European troops dispatched from this country in the summer and autumn must have reached the shores of India—the shores, be it observed; for an arrival at Calcutta or Bombay gives no more assurance of the immediate availability of our forces, than an arrival of stores and provisions at Balaclava used to give of the immediate feeding and clothing of the men before Sebastopol. In this latter instance our difficulty lay in the last seven miles of transit. Now we have distances like these—from Calcutta to Benares is 428 miles; to Allahabad 493 miles; to Cawnpore 628 miles. In these distances is involved the whole matter in question. Men and "matériel" must come up slowly and in driblets, scarcely if at all sufficient to supply the drain caused by the losses which must constantly take place in our small army. Everything depends on reinforcement, and reinforcement is just the difficulty. That it will be overcome of course no one doubts; but that time, great energy, and unflinching activity will be necessary to place our force in a condition to carry on the campaign which is inevitable, is equally beyond a doubt. Nor should we fail to look boldly and truthfully at the fact that the most recent events of which we have heard are calculated to give some heart to the enemy. In a European war a retreat ably and successfully conducted from an untenable position does

DELHI AFTER THE SIEGE: LOOTED HOUSE WITHIN THE PALACE WALLS.

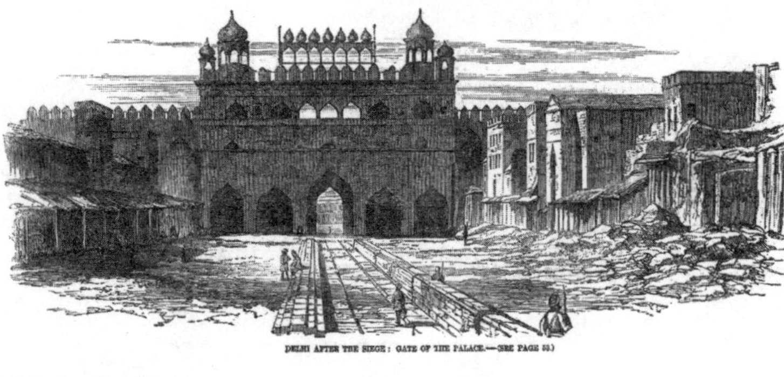

DELHI AFTER THE SIEGE: GATE OF THE PALACE.—(SEE PAGE 53.)

Delhi after the Siege

(*Harper's Weekly*, New York, 21 November 1857, vol. 1, no. 47.)

Courtesy: *Aditi Chandra (Private collection)*

The Azimgarh Proclamation and Some Questions on the Revolt of 1857 in the Northwestern Provinces

During the revolt of 1857 many Indian leaders issued proclamations appealing to their countrymen to support their cause against the British. The Azimgarh proclamation, quoted in full as an appendix to this article, was issued after the seizure of the town in mid-1857 and is among the few documents presenting the Indian side. The present attempt to assess the Azimgarh proclamation is also used as a take-off plank for raising certain questions about the revolt.

The Azimgarh proclamation of 25 August 1857 was issued by a grandson of the Mughal emperor, Bahadur Shah, who was a figurehead stripped of all power. The proclamation documents the subjective aims and ideals of one rebel leader, no doubt in a somewhat exaggerated, if not distorted, manner, due to propaganda needs. There is scope for a separate essay to compare this proclamation with other Indian 1857 proclamations, and to analyse how far its attitude is typical of the entire rebel leadership. Such a detailed survey is not attempted here. It aims not only at rousing 'the wealthy', 'those who have any sort of connection with any of the Mohammedan royal families', the zamindars, merchants, artisans and public servants against the British but also at rousing them for emperor Bahadur Shah. This latter motive gives the document a specific and limited character. It sings the praises of the ousted Mughal family and issues promises. It would appear from this proclamation that the uprising of 1857 was a deep-seated conspiracy on the part of the Mughal emperor. But this was not

This essay appeared in 1976 in *Essays in Honour of Professor SC Sarkar* (Bengal, 1976).

a fact, for Bahadur Shah was more fond of lolling in somnolence than of planning a violent anti-British movement. In fact he was as surprised as the English at the outbreak of the revolt and agreed to take up the nominal leadership with some reluctance.[1]

A TENTATIVE DISTINCTION—VALUE-ORIENTED AND GOAL-ORIENTED MOVEMENTS

Here a digression could be attempted following a recent distinction between value-oriented movements—movements in which the values of the rebels are violently juxtaposed against the values of those in authority—and goal-oriented movements in which the objective is merely the usurpation of political power which leads such rebels to follow the goals of the authority against whom they rise in revolt.[2] Application of this distinction becomes very interesting in the context of 1857, since the rebellion began as an expression of spontaneous outburst of anti-British feeling; the very values of the rebels were different, for they looked askance at all things English. This was the picture when the rebellion was in its very initial stages. After it had progressed, Bahadur Shah appeared to the rebels as the symbol of the imperial past. Re-establishing the *izzat* of the ancestral dynasty now appeared to be most important of all. (It is true, as Professor Sarkar himself has pointed out,[3] that in Awadh, the chief theatre of popular insurrection, the loyalty of the rebels turned to the old local ruling house; but this local ruling house, though formally independent, was very much a part of the Mughal order, which had by now collapsed.) Thus what had started as a spontaneous movement against alien people and institutions incorporated new values, a movement thus value-oriented turned later into fractional movements which merely looked to goals which were traditionalistic.

Having made this oversimplification, we hasten to add that the rebels had no intention of following the goals of the authority which

[1]S.N. Sen, *1857* (Calcutta, 1957), pp. 68–72. Also see Percival Spear, *Twilight of the Mughals* (Cambridge, 1951), pp. 203–4.

[2]I borrow this distinction from Aniruddha Ray, 'Comparative Approaches to the Interpretations of Revolts in late Medieval India' (cyclostyled copy), p. 11; paper read at the seminar on 'Historical Models in the Study of Tradition and Change in India' in October 1969 at the Indian Institute of Advanced Studies, Simla. The paper is due to be published in the IIAS Transactions volume.

[3]Susobhan Sarkar, 'Views on 1857' in *Bengal Renaissance and Other Essays* (New Delhi, 1970), p. 127.

immediately preceded them. The Azimgarh proclamation seems to suggest that undoing all that the British had done was their stated aim. At least some sections of the Indian population were anxious to expel the British from India and were counting days for that fateful event. This is clear from the paragraph in the proclamation where we are told that all religious works of both Hindus and Muslims, astrologers and miracle-workers are agreed that the English will no longer have any footing in India. As this section of the population consisted of the religious men who were respected and honoured in the countryside, it is obvious that many of the peasants believed in the prediction, and were ready to bring about what they thought was god's wish. In the nineteenth century, particularly in the Indian countryside, religion was a vital part of that tradition that conditioned the circumstances in which the rebels had to make their own history. The rebel leaders naturally used religion to organise a movement against an alien government.

ARTISAN PARTICIPATION

The amount of attention and awareness which a proclamation issued by a scion of the Mughal royal family brought up in a somewhat effete cultural atmosphere shows about the decline of Indian artisans and handicrafts under the impact of British rule is perhaps unprecedented in the early and mid-nineteenth century. Even intellectuals like Ram Mohun or Derozio remained oblivious of the extent of de-industrialisation. The annihilation of Indian manufactures was considered too insignificant and unimportant to deserve a place in their thought and writings.[4] The question of the appeal to artisans in the revolts of 1857 opens up new vistas of research since it will definitely be an interesting and fruitful exercise to find out the number of peasants and the number of artisans from among the mass of villagers who did actually participate in the revolt. It should be highlighted here that in the Azimgarh proclamation the solution to the problems of the artisans is that under the *badshahi* government they will 'exclusively be employed in the services of the kings, rajahs and

[4]See Asok Sen, 'The Bengal Economy and Rammohun Roy' (cyclostyled) paper read in the symposium organised by the Nehru Memorial Museum and Library, New Delhi, in October 1972, and to be published in their volume commemorating the bicentenary year of Ram Mohun's birth. And Sumit Sarkar, 'The Complexities of Young Bengal' in *Nineteenth Century Studies* (Calcutta, October 1973).

the rich'; there is no promise of autonomous growth. In this sense the proclamation's attitude to economic life was very much a carry-over of the crisis of the Mughal empire and its dissolution, since one of the basic features of that crisis was the failure of economic life to develop independently by overriding the constraints of politics and religion.[5]

WHY WAS BENGAL DIFFERENT?

The document can mislead us in one respect. It would appear from the proclamation that the mercantile classes joined in the rebellion. There is no doubt that the mercantile classes, urban traders, bankers and moneylenders stood by the foreign rulers. In fact the rebels looked upon them as collaborators of the British for these bankers and moneylenders were made the major subjects of attack in most of the districts of the northwestern provinces.[6]

Historians frequently speculate on what the results of 1857 would have been, had the mercantile classes and the burgeoning Bengali townsfolk joined the revolt. As to how the Bengali baboos reacted to the events of 1857, a brilliant commentary is available in *Hootum Pyanchar Naksha* of Kaliprasanna Sinha (I fear the title of this superb prose piece is rather untranslatable, *Sketches by Hootum* being the common rendering, missing the down-to-earth colloquialism of the Bengali title). The familiar argument that the Bengali baboos kept aloof from the rebellion because they found the ideas of the rebel leaders to be obscurantist and anti-modern is hardly borne out by the proclamation. The proclamation promises steam-vessels for the conveyance of merchandise; this goes against the argument that the introduction of railways was a cause of the outbreak. Moreover the abolition of suttee, another of those handy perennials in the causality of 1857, is not mentioned as a grievance in the proclamation, which mentions so many other concrete grievances. In fact in north India, where Azimgarh was located, and where the revolt tends to get depth of focus, abolition of suttee hardly became a social grievance, unlike Bengal, where the revolt had no social character.

[5]For a clear formulation of this aspect of the Mughal crisis see Asok Sen, 'A Pre-British Economic Formation in India of the late Eighteenth Century: Tipu Sultan's Mysore' (cyclostyled) paper read at a seminar in the Centre for Studies in Social Sciences, Calcutta, 1973.

[6]See Sulekhchandra Gupta, 'Agrarian Background and the 1857 Rebellion in the Northwestern Provinces' in *Enquiry* (no. 1), pp. 69–98.

It is easily comprehensible why the Bengali literati had not welcomed the revolt. The nineteenth-century Bengali intelligentsia, very much a product of the osmosis of English education, was it seems unable to reconcile their borrowed ideal of liberty with the reality of their helplessness and cowardice in the face of a widespread movement. They had already invested themselves in the colonial system and were totally dependent on the British herrenvolk both ideologically and materially. They had completely accepted the false consciousness of the 'do-gooding' influence of British capital and western attitudes in India. Thus they bolstered up alien rule in India and accepted cultural norms which alienated them from the peasants, artisans and the traditional grassroot value systems of the country.[7] They were busy with a kind of dressed-up, spurious bourgeois growth. Events in north India, led by the sort of people who, promulgated the Azimgarh *ishtahar*, were not considered relevant by them for their own growth.

But why did the countryside of Bengal, where the entire production-economy had collapsed[8] since the British started shaking the pagoda tree from 1757, remain quiet and unconnected with the events of 1857. The question becomes more enigmatic when areas of this same province took to arms a few years later when the 'Blue monkeys' were ruining the countryside. Are we to presume then from the quietness of the Bengal countryside in 1857 that the north

[7]All my ideas about the position of the nineteenth-century Bengali intelligentsia vis-a-vis colonialism have been taken from certain papers written recently on various aspects of this theme. The papers are: (a) Asok Sen, 'The Bengal Economy and Rammohun Roy'; (b) Sumit Sarkar, 'Rammohun Roy and the Break with the Past' (cyclostyled) paper read at the above mentioned symposium organised by the Nehru Memorial Museum and Library and to be published in the same volume; (c) Dipesh Chakrabarty, 'The Colonial Context of the Bengal Renaissance: A Note on Early Railway-Thinking in Bengal' (cyclostyled) paper presented at the thirty-third session of the Indian History Congress at Muzaffarpur in December 1972; (d) Barun De, 'A Critique of the Historiography of the Trend Entitled 'Renaissance' in Nineteenth Century India' (cyclostyled) paper presented to the Indo-Soviet symposium on economic and social development of India and Russia from the seventeenth to the nineteenth centuries held at Moscow in May 1973.

It is revealing that the Bengali babus were an object of ridicule among north Indians in 1857. A north Indian described the babus as 'fit only to be employed as attorneys or teachers of Milton and Shakespeare', quoted in S.N. Sen, *op. cit.*, p. 29.

[8]For a brilliant explication of this collapse of Bengal's production-economy see Asok Sen, 'The Bengal Economy and Rammohun Roy'.

and central Indian uprising that year had no deep-seated economic tie-ups with Bengal?[9]

THE LOSS OF PATRONAGE AND THE UPRISING

Regarding public servants, the document rightly points to the lack of influence and the general unimportance of the Indians who were systematically kept out from the higher rungs of official employment. In the executive, the highest post that an Indian could attain was that of deputy collector and that of *sadar-amin* in the judiciary.[10] Vis-a-vis the English, the Indians felt racially inferior and counter-dependent and were discriminated against, even when possessed of equal talents for official service. This was of course immanent in the colonial framework. The attack on racial discrimination in the services was to become a central plank also of later intelligentsia nationalism. This could establish a direct linkage between one aspect of the 1857 revolt and later Indian nationalism.

It is interesting that even according to Sayyid Ahmad Khan—himself a British servant—racial discrimination against the Indians in government services impoverished the people and contributed to the outbreak of 1857.[11] According to him another cause was the abolition of rewards and *jagirs*. In fact, for the courtly retainer as well as for the soldiers in the princely armies who had enjoyed the patronage of the princes before the coming of British rule, Dalhousie's annexations meant the loss of work and patronage. Each annexation extinguished a court and narrowed the areas of Indian employment. Dalhousie's annexations, contrary to British expectations, had caught a Tartar since the annexations turned loose upon the countryside a host of embittered men willing to snatch at any opportunity to oust the men and institutions which had robbed them of patronage and of their source of livelihood. The fate of these men naturally struck a responsive chord in the hearts of their kinsmen in the villages thereby creating a broad base for the rebellion. In the mid-nineteenth century, unlike the late eighteenth century in Bengal, when the Company did give

[9]This point was made by Barun De in his review in *Indian Economic and Social History Review* (New Delhi) of Kling's *The Blue Mutiny* (Philadelphia, 1966).

[10]S.N. Sen, *op. cit.*, p. 31.

[11]For a summary of Sayyid Ahmad Khan's views see Metcalf, *The Aftermath of Revolt* (Princeton, 1964), pp. 88–90.

some opportunity for employment to Bengalis, the Indians were sandwiched between racial discrimination in government service or unemployment after British annexation. It appears however that while the courtly retainers, or men who had enjoyed the patronage of the princes, instinctively threw in their lot with the rebellion, the racially-discriminated government servants—men like Sayyid Ahmad Khan in north India or the professional literati in Bengal, successors of those who had been employed in the late 18th century, and earlier prototypes of men who would later lead intelligentsia nationalism—stood by their British masters.

The proclamation makes a terse statement on the grievances of the zamindars. Historians working on 1857 are mostly agreed that the traditional landholding classes, the zamindars, were the hardest hit by the British innovations in the sphere of land and revenue. The main idea behind the changes which the British introduced in the northwestern provinces[12] was to confer on the right to collect government revenue, a certain prestige, because of which men of wealth and influence would take up the task of revenue collection. The rendering of the right to engage for the government revenue (*malguzari*), alienable and saleable, led to a vast transfer of land rights: and to the displacement of much of the traditional elite, the zamindar, by the urban trading and mercantile classes and moneylenders[13] who were becoming more and more interested in the collection of land-revenue as a profit-making enterprise. British innovations were leading to the creation of a set of parasitic landlords. What M.A. McConaghey wrote in the *Muttra Settlement Report* could apply for all the regions, particularly in the northwestern provinces. McConaghey commented on 'the frightful extent to which hereditary zamindars have been supplanted' between 1833 and 1857 leading to 'the replacement of the hereditary yeoman ... by a body of grasping traders and speculators who are not connected with the soil by ancient traditions, and who look upon the land merely as good capital',[14] In the pre-rebellion decades there

[12]For the changes the British introduced see Sulekhchandra Gupta, see supra note 6.

[13]See Eric Stokes, 'Traditional Elites in the Great Rebellion of 1857: Some Aspects of Rural Revolt in the Upper and Central Doab' in Leach and Mukherjee (eds), *Elites of South Asia* (Cambridge, 1970), pp. 16–32. I have borrowed extensively from Stokes's painstaking research.

[14]M.A. McConaghey, *Muttra Settlement Report*, p. 129; cited in Stokes, *op. cit.*, p. 26.

was a high rate of transfer of proprietary titles; in some districts the rate was as high as 2 per annum. In the district of Aligarh the title to more than 50 per cent of the land changed hands between 1838 and 1858. The moneylending and trading classes registered a gain of 9 per cent between 1839 and 1868.[15] But to presume from the extent of land transfers leading to the displacement of the traditional elite, that they joined the rebellion en bloc would be glossing over the complexities of the situation. If Eric Stokes's researches on the traditional elite in central and upper Doab in 1857 are any index then it would seem that the traditional elite became raggedly split down the middle. Contrary movements occurred in the same region within the same group.

In the district of Meerut the Jats of Hapur pargana fought on the British side while in the Baraut and Barnawa parganas they drove off the British columns and sent supplies to Delhi. In the Muzaffarnagar district, while the Muslim gentry actively supported the Thana Bhawan rising of September 1857, on the other side in the eastern parganas, the Sayyid communities were quiet. The side which the rural populace would take depended on the leadership of the traditional elite. In the Ganges canal tract of Muzaffarnagar the objective conditions all pointed towards rebellion: the traditional elite had lost something like 56 per cent of their land to the urban moneylender between 1840 and 1860. But rebellion was averted by the leadership of a few thriving Sayyid famillies. In southeastern Meerut and the Bulandshahr districts, the Jats followed the lead of the Jat Raja of Kuchesar, Gulab Singh. In Aligarh district where the traditional elite had been severely mauled, 'scarcely one member of the old and powerful families of the district joined in the disturbances: on the contrary some of these gave what assistance they could with undoubted readiness; some, like Thakur Gobind Singh, nobly exposed their lives in our cause, while others afforded and only perhaps because they doubted the policy of refusing ... Strangely enough ... those of the greater families who had lost most by our rule, turned out our firmest friends in the time of trouble and need.'[16] Men like Khairati Khan, of Parasawali in Muzaffarnagar, who placed himself at the head of the Jat rising in 1857 or like Nawab Walidad Khan of Malgarh in the Bulandshahr

[15]W.H. Smith, *Aligarh Settlement Report* (Allahabad, 1862), para 182, p. 65, cited in Stokes, *op. cit.*, pp. 18, 20.

[16]*Aligarh Settlement Report*, para 55, p. 19; cited in Stokes, *op. cit.*, p. 20.

district, under whose banner disaffected Muslim gentry like the Sayyids of Shikarpur rallied,[17] present the other side of the medal. Stokes is of the opinion that men like these were generally lacking in importance. Engels was perhaps right when he remarked that the landlords had come to an agreement with the British and had betrayed the general cause.[18] How far will it be mere speculation to say that the zamindars became apprehensive of the anarchy that came inevitably with the sweep of popular participation, and that they backed out with a policy of thus-far-and-no-further? We await further micro-level studies on the traditional elite in 1857 before such contrary movements within the same group can be made susceptible to historical generalisation.

It will of course be clear that in the data I have used I have depended on research recently done on the northwestern provinces, and have not taken into account the central Indian uprisings, for instance, of Laxmibai of Jhansi or in Sambalpur, or the mutinies in Gujarat. The validity of my questions may be reformulated if research is done on these regions, along the lines opened up by Professor Stokes's and his students' depth surveys.

THE PEASANT AND THE UPRISING

From the proclamation a reader unaccustomed to the events of 1857 may get the impression that the common man of India, the peasant, had hardly anything to do with the uprising. Such an impression will not reflect the facts. This silence regarding peasants is significant as it reveals the attitude of the leaders who possibly regarded the peasants and the sepoys (peasants in uniform) as cannon-fodder (the sepoys are also referred to as plunderers in the third paragraph of the proclamation). This attitude of the leaders may be an indicator of the magnates' fear in the face of lower-class militancy.

The attitude of a *jemadar* of the Awadh artillery as it appeared to Henry Lawrence could go very well as the attitude of the common

[17]All the above facts have been taken from Stokes, *op. cit.*

[18]F. Engels, 'The Revolt in India' (written on 17 September 1858) in Marx and Engels, *The First War of Indian Independence* (Moscow, 3rd edition, 1968), pp. 171–75. It is important to note here, in passing, that though the scattered and densely packed articles on India of Marx and Engels have been published by the Institute of Marxism-Leninism (Moscow) under the above title, Marx and Engels never used the phrase themselves. The *most* Marx would go to was to call the uprising a 'national revolt' (in 'dispatches from India').

man of India towards the English; Lawrence wrote: 'He gave us credit for nothing ... and *hates* us thoroughly.'[19] For all Dalhousie's pity for the peasants,[20] they had probably jumped from the proverbial frying pan into the fire with the coming of British rule. In the northwestern provinces the chief and the most successful theatre of rebellion, the revenue settlements made with the coming of British rule had resulted in extremely heavy assessments. In Aligarh the assessment was 'avowedly based on extracting 80 per cent of the rental assets'.[21] As a natural result of the swinging revenue assessment a large number of cultivating proprietors lost their lands to the trading and moneylending classes. The original cultivators remained in cultivating possession but merely as tenants-at-will. Further for some, it could mean rack-renting, since the proprietors had been given the right to increase the rents of tenants-at-will. These transfers of land, introduction of outsiders and increasing exploitation of the village community, naturally produced wide-spread resentment among the peasants, who were moreover victims of the intrigues of moneylenders, in whose hands the civil courts became instruments of oppression. The resentment was also directed against the institutions of government which had produced such a situation. Together with these changes in agrarian relations several other measures angered the people, e.g. the imposition of the *chowkidari* tax and the appointment of village *chowkidars* were taken as direct tampering with the criminal jurisdiction of the village community and they further aggravated the discontent caused by the transfer of landed property.[22] The village communities were crumbling and every section of rural society had been affected by the British system of land revenue administration. This discontent among all the segments of social strata gave the 1857 rebellion in the northwestern provinces a very large base as well as its strength and intensity. It is highly probable that what is called the 'military causes of the revolt' was just a reflex in the sepoy's mind of the far more fundamental grievances of his kinsmen in the villages.

[19]Quoted in Metcalf, *op. cit.*, p. 48.

[20]See Dalhousie's letter of 5 February 1859 in J.G.A. Baird (ed.), *Private Letters of the Marquess of Dalhousie* (Edinburgh, 1910), p. 399; cited by V.G. Kiernan, 'Marx, Engels and the Indian Mutiny' in P.C. Joshi (ed.), *Homage to Karl Marx* (New Delhi, 1969), p. 110.

[21]Stokes, *op. cit.*, p. 22.

[22]The above facts are taken from Sulekhchandra Gupta, see supra note 6.

Owing to the large base, the outburst naturally acquired a popular character. Examples of popular rebellion are many in any standard account of 1857.[23] Very many detailed strands within the uprising would be found if one differentiated between the various revolts, following the model of Porchnev (elaborated in a series of lectures given by him at the university of Paris, Sorbonne, in 1966; quoted by Dr Aniruddha Ray in the paper referred to earlier in this article; see reference 2) regarding the nature and composition of revolts: (a) vertical movements in which the leadership is with the upper class, while the followers are from the lower class and (b) horizontal movements in which there is practically no determined leadership or the leadership rests with the same class as that of the followers. Both types can be identified in 1857 since zamindars and princes often incited and led the people to insurrection, while spontaneous leaderless bands of rebellious villagers and sepoys are far from uncommon. Dr Ray's point would be that the early value-oriented stage of the movement has, a horizontal, i.e. diffused, leadership or spontaneous base, while in the later goal-oriented stage, vertical, i.e. hierarchical leadership by traditional classes, once in authority but now dispossessed, reasserts itself. Naturally Dr Ray has stated this distinction as a simple model which has to be approximated by detailed research on complexities closer to reality.

The mass of the north Indian population, as George Campbell put it, was 'more or less tinged by rebellion'.[24] In the cities the hoi polloi became a potent revolutionary force; but we also hear of the rural populace rising 'in their thousands'.[25] Popular anti-British feeling in Khair (in Aligarh district) ran so high that the Jats joined their hereditary arch-enemies the Rajputs in open revolt.[26] A very important dimension of these popular outbreaks, though often missed in standard works, was that the 'principal motive in all these acts appears to have been to restore possession of lands lost through the instrumentality of British laws and courts and to wreak vengeance upon those classes who had been the principal beneficiaries'.[27] The objects of rebel wrath and action were the local

[23]For a short but superb discussion on the popular dimensions of the revolt, see Susobhan Sarkar, *op. cit.*, pp. 128–30; also see Metcalf, *op. cit.*, pp. 64–65.

[24]Quoted in Metcalf, *op. cit.*, p. 64.

[25]Stokes, *op. cit.*, p. 18.

[26]Ibid., p. 23.

[27]Sulekhchandra Gupta, see supra note 6, p. 81.

centres of colonial power and the compradore class. The narratives of events attending the outbreak of disturbances which were compiled by the various district officers and divisional commissioners in the northwestern provinces are replete with instances of rebellion against the moneylenders, government *tehsil* buildings and record rooms. In Saharanpur, 'at first the bankers were robbed ... moneylenders and traders were forced to give up their books of accounts, and vouchers for debts ... all the government records with the *mahajuns'* accounts, bonds, etc ... were torn up'. In Muzaffarnagar 'The civil, criminal and collectorate *dufturs* were burnt by the people ... violent crimes of all kinds were committed daily... the *bunyahs* and *mahajuns* were in the majority of cases the victims.' In Aligarh the same story was repeated. In Mathura, 'the confusion and anarchy of the country exceeded belief', the *banias* were plundered, the *tehsil* buildings burnt, together with the 'government buildings on the road, customs *chowkies* and bungalows, police *chowkies* etc.'. Similar facts could also be given from practically all districts of the northwestern provinces.[28]

PERSPECTIVES ON THE CONSEQUENCES OF THE OUTBREAK

It is a major lacuna of Indian historical research that we very often miss the colonial context of 1857. It is a severe drawback that the events of that momentous year are still explained in most works by a set of proximate causes within the 'tradition-modernity' schema. It is important to recall here that a plea was made to break away from such a superficial causal framework back in 1957 by Professor Sushobhan Sarkar in his revealing review-article 'Views on 1857'.[29] There has never been any occasion during the last sixteen years to give up such a plea. Perhaps the only exception is Dr Bipan Chandra's recent book *Modern India*, meant for secondary schools, where he abandons the syndrome of proximate causes for 1857 and analyses the revolt on the broader canvas of India's economic collapse under British rule.[30] Historians in general have been so bogged down by the details of military history of the various battles

[28]Such facts are given by Sulekhchandra Gupta, from which the above instances are also taken.

[29]Susobhan Sarkar, *op. cit.*, p. 128.

[30]Bipan Chandra, *Modern India* (NCERT, New Delhi, 1971), pp. 133–50.

of 1857 and the nature and character of the uprising that an alert student is left wondering about the connection of 1857 with the haphazard and stultified modernisation that India experienced under foreign rule, and also about the precise significance of 1857 in the evolution of post-mutiny British policy.

How far is it correct to hold that the outbreak of 1857 gave such a jolt to the ruling power that the British realised that they could no more rely on the urban literati to bolster up their rule in India; and that the colonial rulers recognised the necessity of going down to the traditional value-system of the country, and 'establishing new normative relations with the broader social strata'?[31] If this view is confirmed then the movement away from the literati after the outbreak could have contributed to the growth of frustration among the literati who had grown up in a collaborative framework within the British Indian pre-mutiny administration. Their new perception of a real subordinate status was discordant with their inheritance of British liberal values. This status-dissonance perhaps led to what Angus Maddison so pithily calls 'step-in-your-shoes nationalism'[32] among the urban intelligentsia and the professional classes in the post-1857 decades. However it would perhaps be going too far to journey the whole way with Dr Seal when he argues that such nationalism was the aping of herrenvolk by sub-elites.[33]

In an earlier paragraph we have noted the tendency of the rebels to attack the local centres of colonial power. Here, an interesting feature is that though the rebels attacked residencies and *tehsil* buildings, they never attacked the real centres of colonial economic domination, like the Gorakhpur sugar mills, or the Kumaon plantations. (In Aligarh though we learn of an instance where some indigo factories were plundered and burnt.)[34] Does this indicate that the outbreak of 1857

[31]Satyesh Chakraborty, 'Split-up Modernization: Its Relevance in the Study of Modern Indian History and Society' (cyclostyled) paper read at the seminar on 'Historical Models in the Study of Tradition and Change in India' in October 1969 at the Indian Institute of Advanced Studies Simla. The paper is due to be published in the IIAS Transactions volume.

[32]Angus Maddison, *Class Structure and Economic Growth* (London, 1971), p. 71.

[33]This is the general attitude of Anil Seal in his *The Emergence of Indian Nationalism* (Cambridge, 1968). See particularly pp. 15–16, 23, 344–46. Note also his snide remark (p. 118), that Bankim Chandra took to novel writing (which as we know was at times anti-British) because he was stuck for eighteen years at the deputy collector rung.

[34]Sulekhchandra Gupta, see supra note 6, p. 84.

had no broader economic tie-up, barring agrarian discontent? Was this lack of broader economic tie-up with the mode of production, which had become decisively colonialised (if there was indeed such a lack) and the failure of the rebels to even think of new 'production-functions' a major cause of the quick suppression of a widespread movement which embraced nearly all segments of the population?

Rebel leadership which was goal-oriented, i.e. trammelled by Mughal vestiges, could hardly have a revolutionary economic programme.

THE REGIONALISATION OF RESISTANCE TO BRITISH RULE

In a study of the expansion of the British empire in India it will be seen that areas tend to make a last-ditch stand against the British immediately after they have been brought under the imperial umbrella; the suppression of that swan song leads to a complete and total absorption of that area within the British empire. Bengal under Mir Kasim, the Marathas in Baji Rao II's later years and the Sikhs under Dalip Singh provide enough data to substantiate the above formulation. Although in the eighteenth century, popular resistance against the Company was lacking in Mir Kasim or Tipu Sultan's wars, yet the guerilla warfare of the northwestern provinces has precursors in the strife which preceded and was crushed in the third Anglo—Maratha war and the second Anglo-Sikh war, both in the early nineteenth century. Can the insurrection of 1857 be fitted into the above formulation, since after all the major theatres of the revolt—Awadh, Rohilkhand, the Doab—had all been annexed by the British a few years before the revolts in these places occurred? It will also be interesting to test the hypothesis that Bengal, Maharashtra and Punjab remained quiet during 1857 since they had already revolted before. We have already noted how the Azimgarh proclamation sang the praises of the Mughal empire. This is perhaps an indicator to the regionalism of the 1857 uprising, to the fact that it was confined mainly to areas which were under the sway of the Mughals even in their declining years.

The Mughal Myth in the Nineteenth Century

Another point deserves scrutiny. In earlier centuries, in the heyday of the Mughal empire, proclamations by Mughal rebels against their own emperors as well as by Rajputs or Marathas who were themselves *watan-jagirdars* of the Mughal empire and aspired to become *zamindaran-i-umda* (patrimony-holding zamindars, who aspired to the status of tributary vassalage), were generally couched in the language of magnates calling on others to maintain traditional liberties within the empire by removing new locusts who were eating away at these liberties,[35] Such statements emphasise not only Hindu traditional liberties but Hindu-Muslim co-existence within the Mughal imperial framework. In the Azimgarh proclamation the following sentence is evocative of that rebellious tradition:

> I who am the grandson of Abul Muzuffer Serajuddin Bahadur Shah Ghazee, King of India, having in the course of circuit come here to ... the eastern part of the country ... have by the aid of the *Majahdeens* (religious warriors), erected the standard of Mohammed, and persuaded the orthodox Hindoos who had been subject to my ancestors, and have been and are still accessories in the destruction of the English, to raise the standard of Mahavir.

It is of course true that here a grandson of the emperor, loyal to him, is purporting to fight usurpers; also, an attempt is being made to affiliate the other imperial tradition, the Marathas (viz 'the standard of Mahavir'). What of course was missing in the earlier documents was the appeal made and attention given, though infructuously, to the mercantile classes, an index perhaps to the new realisation about the importance of the backing of the mercantile community for the success of a rebellion in a colonial situation. But these were due to the circumstances of 1857 as distinct from those of the seventeenth century.

Having drawn a parallel with the Mughals, we point out that the Mughals did not represent the factual sovereigns in the nineteenth century. With the breakdown of Mughal authority in the eighteenth century, there were bred regional loyalties and new focal points of connection in erstwhile Mughal provinces; these new regional territorial entities became germinal points of embryonic patriotism under ambitious magnates.[36] In the late eighteenth

[35]Cases in point are the letters to Aurangzeb complaining against the *jizya* ascribed to Raj Singh by Tod (see Tod, *Annals and Antiquities of Rajasthan*, London, Popular Edition, 1914, vol. I, pp. 302–3) and to Shivaji by Sir J.N. Sarkar (See J.N. Sarkar, *Shivaji*, Calcutta, 1948, pp. 306–9).

[36]See Barun De, 'Some Implications of Political Tendencies and Social Factors in Eighteenth Century India' in O.P. Bhatnagar (ed.), *Studies in Social History (Modern India)*, (Allahahad, 1964), pp. 219, 265.

and nineteenth centuries these territorial units made an effort to oust the imperial power either just before annexation, or pretty soon after being brought under colonial domination. Bengal, Maharashtra and the Punjab had rebelled; in 1857 it was the turn of the northwestern provinces. In these provinces, the traditional imperial (i.e. Mughal, Maratha or Sikh) tradition was the most immediate. That tradition lingered particularly in magnate memory in the northwestern provinces. A revival here of the Mughal myth via magnate leadership was very much on the cards in 1857. Hence the invocation of the Mughals in the proclamation and the tendency to affiliate with the magnate point of view (e.g. zamindars more important than artisans and a contemptuous reference to 'common Ryot, a maidservant or a slave'), It was in this sense, the desire to go back to the disaggregated loose Mughal empire of the eighteenth century, that the uprising was a throwback to the Mughal days. Such an analysis could lend a completely different perspective to the events of 1857.

SOME EMERGING QUESTIONS

At the moment 1857 is a year to conjure with; it remains a very pluralistic phenomenon in which many different shades and strands of rebellion got entangled to proceed cheek by jowl. This is why it is more important to study the events of 1857 in their micro aspects without going adrift from the mainstream of our nineteenth-century history and the fundamental impact of British rule in India. How far is the distinction between value-oriented movements and goal-oriented movements applicable to the events of 1857? If it is, then the transformation from a value-oriented movement in the direction of a goal-oriented movement has to be explained. Studies are necessary to find out the extent of artisan participation in the outbreak. An analysis must be made of the relative quietness of Bengal's countryside in 1857 even though it was the most exploited province. Why did the traditional elite of north India react in different ways in 1857 in spite of the fact that as a set they had suffered most with the coming of British rule? Did the traditional elites in the long run betray the general cause? And a further question: Was there a general cause to be betrayed? If so, what was it? How far did the elite leadership determine which side the rural populace would take? Will any model of differentiating between vertical movements and horizontal movements be useful for unravelling the various strands of the 1857 uprising? What is the precise connection of the insurrection with the thwarted modernization India experienced under colonialism? What is the significance of 1857 in the evolution of post-1857 British policy towards their own dependent intelligentsia? Did the outbreak lead to a movement away from the urban literati and to a recognition of the traditional value-system of the country and of the broader social strata? How far did the above tendency contribute to the emergence of 'step-in-your-shoes nationalism' in the post-1857 decades? Why did the rebels attack the residencies and local centres of imperial power but leave alone the centres of colonial economic domination in north India? Did this indicate a lack of broader economic tie-up and failure on the Indian side to conceive of new production-functions? How far did this shortcoming contribute to the failure of the revolt? Does the revolt of 1857 represent a last-ditch effort on the part of the northwestern provinces stirred by the memory of the Mughals and by regional magnates? Exciting questions crowd round the fateful year. Questions like these make depth studies all the more necessary, for it is through them that a more satisfactory picture of 1857 may emerge. Until more such studies are made it will be a simplistic assessment to use general catch all statements about characteristics and nature to describe the multiplex aspects of 1857.

Appendix
The Azimgarh Proclamation
25 August 1857

It is well known to all, that in this age the people of Hindoostan, both Hindoos and Mohammedans, are being ruined under the tyranny and oppression of the infidel and treacherous English. It is therefore the bounden duty of all the wealthy people of India, especially of those who have any sort of connection with any of the Mohammedan royal families, and are considered the pastors and masters of their people, to stake their lives and property for the well-being of the public. With the view of effecting this general good, several princes belonging to the royal family of Delhi, have dispersed themselves in the different parts of India, Iran, Turan, and Afghanistan, and have been long since taking measures to compass their favourite end; and it is to accomplish this charitable object that one of the aforesaid princes has, at the head of an army of Afghanistan, &c., made his appearance in India; and I, who am the grandson of Abul Muzuffer Serajuddin Bahadur Shah Ghazee, King of India, having in the course of circuit come here to extirpate the infidels residing in the eastern part of the country, and to liberate and protect the poor helpless people now groaning under their iron rule, have, by the aid of the Majahdeens (religious warriors), erected the standard of Mohammed, and persuaded the orthodox Hindoos who had been subject to my ancestors, and have been and are still accessories in the destruction of the English, to raise the standard of Mahavir.

Several of the Hindoo and Mussalman chiefs, who have long since quitted their homes for the preservation of their religion, and have been trying their best to root out the English in India, have presented themselves to me, and taken part in the reigning Indian crusade, and it is more than probable that I shall very shortly receive succours from the West. Therefore, for the information of the public, the present *Ishtahar*, consisting of several sections, is put in circulation, and it is the imperative duty of all to take it into their careful consideration, and abide by it. Parties anxious to participate in the common cause, but having no means to provide for themselves, shall receive their daily subsistence from me; and be it known to all, that the ancient works, both of the Hindoos and the Mohammedans, the writings of the miracle-workers, and the calculation of the astrologers, pundits, and rammals, all agree in asserting that the English will no longer have any footing in India or elsewhere. Therefore it is incumbent on all to give up the hope of the continuation of the British sway, side with me, and deserve the consideration of the Badshai, or imperial Government, by their individual exertion in promoting the common good, and thus attain their respective ends; otherwise if this golden opportunity slips away, they will have to repent of their folly, as it is very aptly said by the poet in two fine couplets, the drift whereof is 'Never let a favourable opportunity slip, for in the field of opportunity you are to meet with the ball of fortune; but if you do not avail yourself of the opportunity that offers itself, you will have to bite your finger through grief.'

No person, at the misrepresentation of the well-wishers of the British Government, ought to conclude from the present slight in conveniences usually attendant on revolutions, that similar inconveniences and troubles should continue when the Badshahi Government is established on a firm basis; and parties badly dealt with by any sepoy or pinderer, should come up and represent their grievances to me, and receive redress at my hands; and for whatever property they may lose in the reigning disorder, they will be recompensed from the public treasury when the Badshahi Government is well fixed.

Section I-Regarding Zemindars. It is evident, that the British Government in making zemindary settlements have imposed exorbitant *Jumas*, and have disgraced and ruined several zemindars, by putting up their estates to public auction for arrears of rent, in so much, that on the institution of a suit by a common Ryot, a maid servant, or a slave, the respectable zemindars are summoned into court, arrested, put in gaol and disgraced. In litigations regarding zemindaries, the immense value of stamps, and other unnecessary expenses of the civil courts, which are pregnant with all sorts of crooked dealings, and the practice of allowing a case to hang on for years, are all calculated to impoverish the litigants. Besides this, the coffers of the zemindars are annually taxed with subscription for schools, hospitals, roads, etc. Such extortions will have no manner of existence in the Badshahi Government; but, on the contrary, the Jumas will be light, the dignity and honour of the zemindars safe, and every zemindar will have absolute rule in his own zemindary ...

Section II-Regarding Merchants. It is plain that the infidel and treacherous British Government have monopolized the trade of all the fine and valuable merchandise, such as indigo, cloth, and other articles of shipping, leaving only the trade of trifles to the people, and even in this they are not without their share of the profits, which they secure by means of customs and stamp fees, &c. in *money* suits, so that the people have merely a trade in name. Besides this, the profits of the traders are taxed, with postages, tolls, and subscriptions for school &c. Notwithstanding all these concessions, the merchants are liable to imprisonment and disgrace at the instance or complaint of a worthless man. When the Badshahi Government is established, all these aforesaid fraudulent practices shall be dispensed with, and the trade of every article, without exception, both by land and water, shall he open to the native merchants of India, who will have the benefit of the Government steam-vessels and steam-carriages for the conveyance of their merchandise gratis; and merchants having no capital or their own shall be assisted from the public treasury.

It is therefore the duty of every merchant to take part in the war, and aid the Badshahi Government with his men and money, either secretly or openly, as may be consistent with his position or interest, and forswear his allegiance to the British Government.

Section Ill-Regarding Public Servants. It is not a secret thing, that under the British Government, natives employed in the civil and military services have little respect, low pay, and no manner of influence; and all the posts of dignity and emolument in both the departments are exclusively bestowed on Englishmen, for natives in the military service, after having devoted the great for part of their lives, attain to the post of soobadar (the very height of their hopes) with a salary of 60r. or 70r. per mensem; and those in the civil service obtain the post of Sudder Ala, with a salary of 500r. a month, but no influence, jagheer, or present ...

Therefore, all, the natives in the British service ought to be alive to their religion and interest, and, abjuring their loyalty to the English, side with the Badshahi Government, and obtain salaries of 200 or 300 rupees per month for the present, and be entitled to high posts in future. If they, for any reason, cannot at present declare openly against the English, they can heartily wish ill to their cause, and remain passive spectators of passing events, without taking any active share therein. But at the same time they should indirectly assist the Badshahi Government, and try their best to drive the English out of the country ...

Section IV-Regarding Artisans. It is evident that the Europeans, by the introduction of English articles into India, have thrown the weavers, the cotton dressers, the carpenters. the blacksmiths, and the shoemakers, &c, out of employ, and have engrossed their occupations, so that every description of native artisan has been reduced to beggary. But under the Badshahi Government the native artisans will exclusively be employed in the services of the king's, the rajahs, and the rich; and this will no doubt ensure their prosperity. Therefore these artisans ought to renounce the English services, and assist the *Majahdeens*, engaged in the war, and thus be entitled both to secular and eternal happiness.

Section V-Regarding Pundits, Fakirs and Other Learned Persons. The pundits and fakirs being the guardians of the Hindoo and Mohammedan religions respectively, and the Europeans being the enemies of both the religions, and as at present a war is raging against the English on account of religion, the pundits and fakirs are bound to present themselves to me, and take their share in the holy war ...

Lastly, be it known to all, that whoever, out of the abovenamed classes, shall after the circulation of this *Ishtahar*, still cling to the British Government, all his estates shall be confiscated, and his property plundered, and he himself, with his whole family, shall be imprisoned, and ultimately put to death.

The text of the Azimgarh Proclamation is taken from Ainslee T. Embree (ed.), 1857 *in India: Mutiny or War of Independence?* (Boston, 1963) in Problems in Asian Civilization series.

Angel of Mercy
Courtesy: *Wiki Commons*

To commemorate those who had been killed in the Bibighur and whose bodies had been thrown into a well, the British erected a statue of the Angel of Mercy over the well and surrounded it by a garden. The site was made sacred and no Indian was allowed to visit it. The protest against this came on Independence Day 1947 when a crowd rushed in and damaged the nose of the Angel. The statue was later removed and kept in an adjoining museum.

'Satan Let Loose Upon Earth': The Kanpur Massacres in India in the Revolt of 1857

> In fact, the peculiar aggravation of the Cawnpore massacres was this, that the deed was done by a subject race—by black men who dared to shed the blood of their masters, and that of poor helpless ladies and children. Here we had not only a servile war and a sort of Jacquerie combined, but we had a war of religion, a war of race, and a war of revenge, of hope, of national promptings to shake off the yoke of a stranger, and to re-establish the full power of native chiefs, and the full sway of native religions ... Whatever the causes of the mutiny and the revolt, it is clear enough that one of the modes by which the leaders, as if by common instinct, determined to effect their end was, the destruction of every white man, woman or child who fell into their hands.[1]

'Our learned men ... told us that the Company's rule would come to an end in 1857, since this was one hundred years after the Company's first great battle': so wrote Sitaram, the loyal sepoy, in his autobiographical narrative of the uprising of 1857.[2]

This article was first published as '"Satan Let Loose Upon the Earth": The Kanpur Massacres in India in the Revolt of 1857' (*Past and Present*, August 1990, Number 128).

[1]W.H. Russell, *My Indian Mutiny Diary* (ed. M. Edwardes) (New York, 1970), pp. 29–30.

[2]Sitaram, *From Sepoy to Subedar* (ed. James Lunt, trans. Captain Norgate) (London, 1970), p. 173. The proclamation of Bahadur Shah, dated 25 August 1857, noted that—'the ancient works, both of the Hindoos and the Mahommedans, the writings of the miracle workers, and the calculations of the astrologers, pundits and rammals, all agree in asserting that the English will no longer have any footing in

The explosion that the astrologers had predicted—a prophecy that was widely circulated in north India—did indeed come, but not exactly on the centenary of Plassey. It began on 10 May 1857 in the cantonment town of Meerut, north-east of Delhi.[3] In the space of one month the uprising had engulfed the entire Gangetic plain, and British rule there, as one British officer put it, had collapsed 'like a house made of cards'.[4] It took nearly two years for British rule to be re-established. The uprising and the subsequent re-establishment of British power were marked by scenes of violence quite unparalleled in the history of British rule in India. This article attempts to analyse one such episode: the massacres of the British by the rebel Indians in Kanpur (Cawnpore).

Violence, it must be emphasized, was an essential component of the British presence in India. It was violence that served as the ultimate imprimatur of colonialism. 'There was no power in India', wrote Philip Francis, 'but the power of the sword, and that was the British sword, and no other'. Francis's famous rival, Warren Hastings, also admitted that the sword was the most valid title the British had to sovereignty in India.[5] A dominant power is always uneasy with violence directed against it, since non-reciprocal violence is one of the necessary conditions of its reproduction. The right to violence is, therefore, everywhere a privilege that authority enjoys and refuses to share with those under it: power always insists on violence as its exclusive monopoly. British rule in India, as an autocracy, had meticulously constructed a monopoly of violence. The revolt of 1857 shattered that monopoly by matching an official, alien violence by an indigenous violence of the colonized.

The violence associated with British power also manifested itself in crude forms, since British rule and domination in India had a very physical aspect. It chose the body as the site to inscribe

---

India or elsewhere': quoted in S.A. Rizvi and M. Bhargava (eds), *Freedom Struggle in Uttar Pradesh*, 6 vols (Lucknow, 1960), i, pp. 453 ff.

[3]A detailed reconstruction of the Meerut outbreak is available in J.A.B. Palmer, *The Mutiny Outbreak at Meerut in 1857* (Cambridge, 1966).

[4]Martin Gubbins, *An Account of the Mutinies in Oudh and the Siege of the Lucknow Residency* (London, 1858), p. 118.

[5]R. Guha, *A Rule of Property for Bengal* (Paris and The Hague, 1963; repr. Calcutta, 1982), p. 146.

its superiority. The bodies of the British acquired certain dignities in India that were predestined by birth and by the colour of their skin. This was the condition of their domination, of their superiority: rulers and ruled were arranged hierarchically as superior and inferior races, as civilized and uncivilized. And this superiority manifested itself by denying to the Indians a 'humanness'; by treating them and conceiving of them as animals. William Howard Russell, the *Times* correspondent, noted in his diary that:

> to the intelligent Briton, they are as the beasts of the field. 'By Jove! sir', exclaims the major, who has by this time got to the walnut stage of the argument, to which he has arrived by gradations of sherry, port, ale and Madeira,—'By Jove!' he exclaims, thickly and fiercely, with every vein in his forehead swoln like whip cord, 'those niggers are such a confounded sensual lazy set, cramming themselves with ghee and sweetmeats and smoking their cursed chillumjees all day and all night, that you might as well think to train pigs ...' The fact is, I fear that the favourites of heaven—the civilizers of the world—*la race blanche* ... are naturally the most intolerant in the world.[6]

Another British resident recorded that:

> the sepoy is [regarded as] an inferior creature. He is sworn at. He is treated roughly. He is spoken as a 'nigger'. He is addressed as 'suar' or pig, an epithet most approbrious to a respectable native ... [the younger British officers] seem to regard it as an excellent joke, as an evidence of spirit and a praiseworthy sense of superiority over the sepoy to treat him as an inferior animal.[7]

It was an era of brutal floggings and of Indian women being forced to become mistresses of white men; of recalcitrant elements being blown from cannons so that their bodies were effaced and the onlookers covered with blood and fragments of flesh. British rule thus visibly manifested itself by marking the body of the Indian. This brutality and violence is important if we are to understand the overall context of the Kanpur massacres. Imperial rule in India

[6]Russell, *My Indian Mutiny Diary*, p. 8.

[7]Quoted in C. Hibbert, *The Great Mutiny: India, 1857* (Harmondsworth, 1978), p. 56.

could only perpetuate itself by a deployment of terror, a terror that would strike awe in the minds of the ruled.

The British had not only conquered India but had also, in the process of consolidating their power in the first half of the nineteenth century, violated all that was held sacred and dear by the people of India. Social reforms based on the principles of reason, land-revenue administration based on Ricardian theories of rent, a legal system imported from England, the propagation of Christianity and the dispossession of kings, their successors and landed magnates, had together brought about a major upheaval in north India. An entire way of life was going under, and naturally the people affected felt aggrieved. This way of life in the nineteenth century was inevitably imbricated with religion. The reforming zeal of British administrators was thus often interpreted as an attempt to subvert the religion of Hindus and Muslims. This created an atmosphere of fear and distrust in which anything associated with Christianity was an object of suspicion and hatred. In Sitapur, in Awadh, the very name of the commissioner—Mr Christian—became identified with the religion and increased the wrath of the rebels.[8] The uprising of 1857 thus displayed a very strong religious fervour. The rebels thought that they were fighting in defence of their religion. And in this there was no difference between a Hindu and a Muslim.[9] A group of rebels setting out why they had taken to arms declared, 'If the religion of a Hindoo or Mussalman is lost, what remains in the world'?[10] A rebel proclamation announced that 'The rebellion began with religion'.[11]

There was among the people and the sepoys a deep-seated belief in the existence of a deliberate British plot to overthrow caste and

[8]J.W. Kaye, *History of the Sepoy War in India, 1857–58*, 3 vols (London; i, 9th edn., 1880; ii, 5th edn., 1881; iii, 4th edn., 1880), iii, p. 456.

[9]The religious fervour and unity are discussed in R. Mukherjee, *Awadh in Revolt, 1857–58: A Study of Popular Resistance* (Delhi, 1984), pp. 147–54.

[10]National Archives of India, Delhi, Foreign Dept., Political Consultations, 13 May 1859, consultation no. 326, abstract translation of an *arzi* (proclamation) from the rebel camp on the part of all the rebel officers and sepoys to Maharaja Jang Bahadur, n.d.: quoted in Rizvi and Bhargava (eds), *Freedom Struggle*, ii, pp. 603–5.

[11]National Archives of India, Foreign Dept., Political Consultations, 17 Dec. 1858, consultation no. 251, 'Translation of a Proclamation Issued by the Begum in the Name of Birjis Qadr'.

religion. The interventions of British administrators in all aspects of life only served to aggravate these apprehensions. Such an atmosphere facilitated the circulation of rumours. In north India in the summer of 1857, there were rumours about the cartridges of the new Enfield rifle being coated with the fat of cows and pigs; about flour being polluted by bone-dust; about forcible conversions to Christianity; about the intentions of the British to disarm the sepoys; and about the end of British rule at the centenary of Plassey. All these circulating together aggregated into one gigantic rumour about the evil intentions of the British. Untraceable in their origin and unverifiable in their import, the rumours moved in a powerful current touching on issues that were profoundly close to indigenous sentiments. What was important in all this was not the objective truth, but what the people believed to be true. And it was this belief that bred fear and panic. Rumour spread from village to village, from bazaar to bazaar and from one sepoy line to another, bringing men together, stoking their suspicion and hatred and thereby spurring them to violent action.[12]

The violence intrinsic to British rule in India, the violation by zealous British administrators of all that was sacred and cherished, and a perceived threat to religion that manifested itself in the circulation of rumours—these are perspectives that have to be borne in mind for comprehending the nature of the uprising and the massacres in Kanpur.

* * *

The first news of disaffection among the sepoys of the Bengal Army reached Kanpur some time in April 1857.[13] In May the news of the outbreak in Meerut and, following that, the fall of

[12]For rumours, see Mukherjee, *Awadh in Revolt*, pp. 72–76; for a more general discussion on rumours in peasant insurgency, see R. Guha, *Elementary Aspects of Peasant Insurgency in Colonial India* (Delhi, 1983), pp. 251–77.

[13]Deposition of Sheo Churrun Das, Sadho of Cawnpoor, in *Depositions taken at Cawnpore under the Direction of Lieutenant-Colonel* G.W. *Williams* (hereafter *Depositions at Cawnpore)*, printed with *Narrative of the Events in the NWP in 1857–58* (Calcutta, n.d.), section on Kanpur (hereafter *Narrative, Kanpur)*. See also G. Williams, 'Review of the Evidence Taken at Cawnpore Regarding the Revolt at that Station in June and July 1857' (hereafter 'Review of the Evidence'), in *Narrative, Kanpur.*

Delhi a few days later, had an electrifying effect on the troops and the population in Kanpur as well as all over north India. As one officer put it:

> The intelligence received of the mutiny of the troops at Meerut appears to have lit the flame at Cawnpore, as well as at every other station it reached. So daring an act of mutiny with murder of their Officers in the presence of an overwhelming European force—the repetition of the same at Delhi—the seizure of that City with the proclamation of a rebel king, encouraged and strengthened the hands of the disaffected amongst the native troops and other classes in the station and neighbourhood.[14]

Troops in Kanpur very soon began to show their hostility to the British. One sepoy told an employee at the commissariat, 'You are serpents, and not one of you shall be spared'.[15] In the bazaar a sergeant's wife was told by a sepoy out of regimental dress, 'You will none of you come here much oftener; you will not be alive another week'.[16] There was a general sense of alarm and expectancy in the city, in which there also seemed to be more sepoys and villagers than usual.[17] In the sepoy lines, *panchayats* (a general assembly where things of importance are discussed and decided collectively) were held every night.[18] A loyal sepoy made the following statement after the revolt:

> The foremost in this consultation [held on 4 June) were Shumsh-ood-deen Khan, Sheikh Boolagee, Sirdar Beg, Raw Singh and others ... The meetings were held at Shumsh-ood-deen's house, and sometimes at the house of Teeka Ram Singh, a subadar of the cavalry ... On the 4th June, all the troopers sent away their families and property to the city.[19]

The mutiny began on the night of 4 June 1857 in what J.W. Kaye described as the 'wonted fashion': firing of guns and extensive

[14] Williams, 'Review of the Evidence'.

[15] W.J. Shepherd, *A Personal Narrative or the Outbreak and Massacre at Cawnpore, during the Sepoy Revolt of 1857* (Lucknow, 1879), p. 11.

[16] Mowbray Thomson, *The Story of Cawnpore* (London, 1859), p. 29.

[17] Nanak Chand's diary of events in Kanpur (hereafter Nanak Chand's diary), printed as 'Translation of a Narrative of Events at Cawnpore', in *Narrative, Kanpur:* 3 June 1857.

[18] C. Ball, *History of the Indian Mutiny*, 2 vols (London, n.d.), i, pp. 299–300.

[19] Deposition of Ewuz Khan, in *Depositions at Cawnpore*.

burning of British property.[20] Then the sepoys sped in the direction of Delhi, stopping for the night at a place called Kalyanpur, a little distance from Kanpur.

Since the time of the outbreak at Meerut, the British in Kanpur had been making preparations to protect themselves. Sir Hugh Wheeler, commander of the Kanpur Division, a favourite of the sepoys and convinced of the loyalty of his troops, decided none the less to take precautions. He was responsible not only for the safety of the British troops and their families, but also of all Europeans. He decided, principally because he did not want to be too distant from the sepoy lines, not to use the magazine adjacent to the river and which, surrounded by a strong wall, was therefore the best suited as a defensive position. Instead he chose a spot nearer the sepoy lines, where there were two single-storied barracks with verandahs around them and several outhouses. This site he began to entrench, to fortify with artillery and stock with provisions. As the alarm spread in the city he ordered all Europeans into the entrenchment, which came to be inhabited by some nine hundred persons.[21] This would be the spot where the British would remain until 27 June. Surrounded on all sides by rebels who fired on them night and day, the British withstood the siege. Their suffering and heroism are the stock-in-trade of most popular accounts of the Mutiny.[22]

From Kalyanpur the rebels turned back, having first met up with Nana Sahib and his men. Nana Sahib was the adopted son of the last *peshwa* (prime minister), Baji Rao II, the leader of the Maratha confederacy, who had surrendered to the English in June 1818. In retirement with an annual pension of £80,000 from the East India Company, the former *peshwa* lived in Bithur, a little distance away from Kanpur. He adopted three sons; Nana Sahib, or Dhondo Pant, which was his real name, was the eldest. In his will Baji Rao made Nana Sahib the sole heir to his property. When Nana Sahib inherited the property after Baji Rao's death in 1851 he

[20] Kaye, *History of the Sepoy War*, ii, p. 307.

[21] Shepherd, *Personal Narrative of the Outbreak and Massacre at Cawnpore*, p. 19.

[22] See, for example, Hibbert, *Great Mutiny*, ch. 9; S.N. Sen, *1857* (Delhi, 1957). The best contemporary accounts are Shepherd, *Personal Narrative of the Outbreak and Massacre at Cawnpore*; Thomson, *Story of Cawnpore*. A nineteenth-century reconstruction is available in G.O. Trevelyan, *Cawnpore* (first pubd. 1865; repr. Brentwood, 1986); references are to the reprint.

was in his thirties. The Company's government, however, refused to recognize his right to the pension that Baji Rao had received. 'For thirty years', the governor-general wrote, 'the Peishwa received an annual stipend ... Those who remain have no claim whatever on the consideration of the British Government'. The Nana Sahib appealed to the court of directors and even sent his agent, Azimullah, to London to plead his case. His efforts were in vain. Yet he continued to remain friendly with the British, entertaining them quite lavishly in his palace in Bithur.[23] His relationship with them was so close that he was invited by the magistrate of Kanpur to guard the treasury; Nana Sahib had, in fact, put himself 'in frequent communication with the Magistrate ... and proffered offers of assistance in case of an outbreak'.[24] The circumstances that led to Nana Sahib's joining the rebels will be discussed below. Suffice to say at this point of the narrative that the rebels returned to Kanpur and the Nana informed General Wheeler on 7 June of his intention to attack the British entrenchment. The siege had begun.

On 25 June the British pickets saw a woman approaching the entrenchments. The identity of the woman is somewhat of a mystery: eyewitnesses identify her as either Mrs Greenway or Mrs Jacobi. She carried a letter which stated that 'All those who are in no way connected with the acts of Lord Dalhousie, and are willing to lay down their arms, shall receive a safe passage to Allahabad'.[25] It was not signed, but the handwriting was recognized as Azimullah's. Negotiations began, terms of surrender were agreed upon and the treaty signed by Nana Sahib. The conditions of surrender, according to Mowbray Thomson, were 'honourable surrender of our shattered barracks and free exit under arms, with sixty rounds of ammunition per man; carriages to be provided for the conveyance of the wounded, the women and children; boats furnished with flour

[23]The best account of Nana Sahib is in P. C. Gupta, *Nana Sahib and the Rising at Cawnpore* (Oxford, 1963). The Governor-General's letter is quoted on p. 20.

[24]J. W. Sherer, 'Some Accounts of the Mutiny and Subsequent Events at Cawnpore', in *Narrative, Kanpur.* Zoe Yolland suggests in *Traders and Nabobs: The British in Cawnpore, 1765–1857* (Salisbury, 1987), pp. 251, 318–19 n. 38, that the trust reposed in Nana Sahib by the British was a consequence of the family ties between him and General Wheeler's 'unofficial wife, an Indian lady'.

[25]India Office Library and Records, London (hereafter I.O.L.R.), Papers of General Sir Mowbray Thomson, Photo Eur 137.

to be ready at the *ghaut* [embankment]'.[26] On the morning of 27 June the British left the entrenchments to proceed to Satichaura Ghat, where the boats were kept. According to one estimate, made after comparing different accounts, four hundred and fifty persons came out of the entrenchments.[27] As the British began to board the boats, guns opened fire from both banks and the thatched awnings of the boats were set alight. All but one hundred and thirty were slaughtered; twenty of the survivors managed to escape, the rest were taken prisoner.

To appreciate the nature of this massacre some features of the outbreak in Kanpur have to be highlighted. In Kanpur, as in most other stations of north India, when the sepoys took recourse to direct action the first targets of destruction were the government buildings, the telegraph wires, the post office, the court, the jail and the record rooms. All those buildings that represented the presence of British rule were burnt or demolished. Similarly, British-owned bungalows—buildings unlike any kind of Indian residence—were objects of the rebels' fury. More significantly, as the mutinies commenced, the sepoys 'divest[ed] themselves of their uniform', tore off the regimental colours and broke out from their lines.[28] As three sepoys giving evidence to the British said, 'the men [sepoys] did as they liked. No, they did not dress in uniform'.[29] In the moment of mutiny the sepoys cast off the markers with which an alien power had sought to regiment them and thus set them apart from the peasantry from which they were recruited. Of course the one marker they would not jettison was their arms. The 'peasant in uniform'—as the sepoy was—disowned his uniform only to become the peasant with arms. In eschewing the regimental discipline that the British officers had drilled into them they reclaimed their peasant character. They merged with the ordinary people.

This merger is significant since it signals the extension of the mutinies to a general uprising. The mutinies struck with

[26]Thomson, *Story of Cawnpore*, p. 153.

[27]Shepherd, *Personal Narrative of the Outbreak and Massacre at Cawnpore*, p. 74.

[28]'Synopsis of the Evidence of the Cawnpore Mutiny' (hereafter 'Synopsis'), in *Narrative, Kanpur;* see also G.W. Forrest, *Selections from the Letters, Despatches and other State Papers Preserved in the Military Department of the Government of India, 1857–58* (hereafter *Selections*), 4 vols (Calcutta, 1893–1912), ii, introduction, pp. 156–58.

[29]Depositions of Gobind Singh, Sheikh Elahee Buksh and Ghouse Mohomed, in *Depositions at Cawnpore.*

remarkable success resulting in the disappearance of British rule in north India. This breakdown allowed the inhabitants of Kanpur's neighbouring villages, some of whom had been arming themselves prior to the mutiny, to pour into the city.[30] Once this happened it became meaningless and impossible to distinguish the rebel and the mutineer. Insurgency, true to its character, had become a collective enterprise.[31] Nanak Chand, a loyalist who kept a diary of the events in Kanpur and scrupulously recorded names whenever he could, pointed to this, albeit unconsciously, when he wrote on 6 June, 'There is a great crowd. It is impossible to record the names of all at such a time'. And again we read in the entry for 8 June, 'It would be impossible to mention the names of all evil-minded men who joined the standard'.[32] Sheer numbers led the diarist to despair, but for historians the anonymity, the facelessness of the thousands involved, is indicative of the collective nature of the project.

An *émeute* within the army had acquired the character of an insurgency almost as soon as it occurred. The populace, seized by a rebel consciousness, set out to destroy, but not indiscriminately. The British, and all that they owned or represented, were the first target. After this the destruction extended to the wealthy and propertied in Kanpur; businessmen, especially money-lenders, were the chief targets.[33] Such discrimination and selectivity in destruction has been singled out as one of the general features of peasant insurgency in colonial India.[34] The destruction in Kanpur was carried out by ordinary people, members of the lower orders of society. This is clear from Nanak Chand's frequent use of words like 'bad characters', *budmashes*, and 'low-caste men'; there are also clear references to villagers and artisans.[35] Lala Badri Nath, the commissariat contractor in Kanpur, also testified that 'Thousands of the lower classes from the city, cantonments and villages went about with them sharing in their excesses'.[36] The uprising in

[30]Nanak Chand's diary: 29, 31 May, 3, 5 June, 1857.

[31]Insurgency and collectivity is analysed in great depth in Guha, *Elementary Aspects of Peasant Insurgency*, *passim*, esp. ch. 4.

[32]Nanak Chand's diary: 6, 8 June 1857.

[33]Ibid.: 5, 6 June 1857.

[34]Guha, *Elementary Aspects of Peasant Insurgency*, pp. 20 ff.

[35]Nanak Chand's diary: 5,6 June 1857.

[36]Deposition of Lala Badri Nath, in *Depositions at Cawnpore*.

Kanpur bore the imprint of the subaltern classes: Nanak Chand was emphatic about this by declaring 'not one of the respectable citizens joined the Jehad'.[37] Respectability, needless to add, was defined in the eyes of Nanak Chand, as well as the British, by the ownership of wealth and property. The men of property saw the rebellion as the work of the subaltern classes and the latter made it their own by their very actions. Two overlapping structures of domination—overlapping because most traders and money-lenders in nineteenth-century India, who were the rebels' targets, earned their profits by collaborating with the British—were simultaneously attacked by the subordinated. In confronting the structures of domination directly the rebels defined their task as a project of power.

It was not just direct action that informed the project. Other features of insurgency, like undermining the prestige of the dominators through verbal and other kinds of insult, accompanied the outbreak. Shepherd recalled that while in captivity he had been continously insulted and that the rebels would not utter a word without an 'abusive epithet' to describe the British.[38] Amelia Horne recorded the 'rude and rough' behaviour of the rebels when they entered the entrenchments on the morning of 27 June. British officers, she said, were severely beaten, and when an officer objected to such behaviour 'they abused him in so gross a manner that it made the ears of all tingle, threatening in the bargain to spit on his face'. The British were not accustomed to such behaviour; it frightened 'us to death', wrote Amelia Horne.[39] The women who were taken as prisoners from the site of the massacre were often taken out to grind corn; in his magisterial narrative of the 'Sepoy War', Kaye, with great discernment, observes that:

> An educated English gentlewoman needed not even a week's residence in India to teach her the meaning of this. As they sat

[37]Nanak Chand's diary: 7 June 1857. By 'Jehad' he is referring to the raising of the green flag.

[38]Shepherd, *Personal Narrative of the Outbreak and Massacre at Cawnpore*, pp. 81–84.

[39]British Lib., London (hereafter Brit. Lib.), Add. MS. 41488, Papers relating to the Indian Mutiny, i, Amy Haine's [Amelia Horne?] Narrative. The same narrative with minor additions and alterations is reprinted as Amelia Bennett [née Horne?], 'Ten Month's Captivity after the Massacre at Cawnpore', in *The Nineteenth Century* (Jan.-June 1913), pp. 1212–34; ibid. (July-Dec. 1913), pp. 78–91. There was no Amelia Bennett in the Kanpur entrenchment so this is in all probability the narrative of Amelia Horne, who escaped the massacre.

> there on the ground, these Christian captives must have had some glimmering recollection of their biblical studies, and remembered how in the East the grinding of corn was ever regarded as a symbol of subjection.[40]

An act carried out every day by a peasant woman in India would indeed be the utmost humiliation when imposed upon a woman of the master race. Colonel Ewart, before being killed, was taunted by the former sepoys of his regiment as the British walked out of the entrenchment with the words, 'Is not this a fine parade and is it not well dressed up?'[41] The British were certainly not used to being taunted or insulted; they expected deference and obedience. It was only in the circumstances of rebellion, when the established relationship of domination and subordination had been broken, that the codes of behaviour could be so grossly violated.

It was not the British alone who had such indignities inflicted upon them. The elites of Kanpur, who were known to be friends of the British, were similarly insulted. The Nuneh Nawab, or Mahomed Ali Khan, an influential person in the town and a known friend of the British, had his horse taken away from him and 'instead of which I got a mere 'Tuttoo' [mare/mule] belonging to a servant of my brother'.[42] In a society where the type of carriage invariably indicated status, to ask a Nawab to ride a mule—and that belonging to a servant—was to destroy his position in society. The Nuneh Nawab was also 'led through the streets in ignominious show', the rebels 'heaped abuses on me' and 'threatened to have me tied to a tree'.[43]

As the rebellion gathered momentum the ranks of the rebels swelled. People came 'to see the fun' of the dominators being attacked and humiliated, and such people were pressed into the rebellion.[44] The rebels used their presence in large numbers to win over the vacillator and draw the onlooker into the folds of the rebellion. Numbers provided the moral prestige of solidarity:

[40]Kaye, *History of the Sepoy War, 1857–58*, ii, p. 355.

[41]'Synopsis'.

[42]I.O.L.R., Board's Collection, no. 195724, translation of the diary of the Nuneh Nawab.

[43]Ibid.

[44]Nanak Chand's diary: 7 June 1857.

collectivity afforded a sanction for those less willing to join.[45] The collective nature of the enterprise possibly contributed to it being seen as 'fun': there was feasting and *sharbat* (sherbet) was distributed;[46] the rebels held nautches with buffoons.[47] There was a sense of liberation, the joy of having achieved the impossible.

What these features make obvious is that the initiative for the uprising in Kanpur came from the ordinary people. Having revolted and destroyed, they still had to deal with Nana Sahib. There are two versions of the meeting between the rebels and the Nana. According to one version, a deputation from the rebels met and told him, 'Maharaj, a kingdom awaits you if you join our cause but death if you side with our enemies'. The Nana readily replied, 'What have I to do with the British? I am altogether yours'. And in a royal gesture he placed his hands on their heads and swore to join them. The other version states that when the Nana saw the entire soldiery had completely thrown off their allegiance to the Company, he decided to join and advise them.[48]

In a case like this there is no way of establishing through the historian's standard methods of cross-checking which is the correct version. But both the accounts convey one important aspect. The Nana did not have very much of a choice. In the one version, the absence of choice was direct: the rebels made it clear that death was the alternative. In the other, the lack of choice was not so direct. Yet, surrounded by an insurgent population eager to embark on a career of destruction, the Nana could only have courted death and destruction by opposing the rebels. Having his own grievances against the British, he considered it prudent to throw in his lot with the insurgents. At that moment, with British power virtually non-existent and an entire populace up in arms, Nana Sahib had no alternative but to join the rebels. In short he was a prisoner of the circumstances. Perhaps this was what Tantia Topi, a very close associate of Nana Sahib, wanted to indicate when, in his confession to the British, he said that after the mutiny 'the three Regiments of Infantry and 2nd Light Cavalry surrounded us and imprisoned

[45]'Pressing' as an instrument of solidarity is discussed in Guha, *Elementary Aspects of Peasant Insurgency*, pp. 195–98.

[46]Nanak Chand's diary: 8 June 1857.

[47]Deposition of John Fitchett, in *Depositions at Cawnpore.*

[48]See Forrest, *Selections*, ii, introduction, pp. 158–59.

the Nana and myself'.[49] There is no evidence whatsoever of either Nana Sahib or Tantia Topi ever being held prisoner. The statement can then only be read as a testimony of helplessness in the face of popular insurgency pressing Nana Sahib into the rebellion. Such a situation was not at all unique in 1857. Time and time again, in different regions, deposed rulers and dispossessed landed magnates were forced to rebel because of the mounting pressure around them. The old and retired Mughal emperor was forced to accept the nominal leadership of the rebellion by the sepoys from Meerut and the populace of Delhi; in Jhansi, the rani became a rebel leader because all around her there were rebels coercing her to join; in Bihar, in Jagdishpur, the eighty-year-old Kunwar Singh had the mantle of rebel leader thrust upon him; and in Awadh the big landed magnates joined or stayed with the rebellion because of the militancy of their peasantry.[50] It would, however, be an over-simplification to suggest that princes and magnates joined the rebellion only because they were forced to by pressure from below. Many of the older ruling class had their own reasons for being antagonistic towards the British. The latter had taken away their power, prestige and land. The uprising offered a unique conjuncture when elite disaffection and popular insurgency could come together.

The significant question is, of course, why the rebels needed a man like Nana Sahib or the Mughal emperor. The answer lies in the rebels' quest for legitimacy. The rebellion wanted to affirm itself in the name of a public authority. Having destroyed, they now wanted to reconstitute the world. And that reconstitution in nineteenth-century India and in the context of the rebel consciousness was not possible, alas, outside the world of hierarchy. The rebel consciousness thus sought to legitimize its actions by appealing to a leader, a king. It harked backed to an older political system—the declining Mughal empire of the eighteenth century,

[49]I.O.L.R., Home Miscellaneous, no. 727 A, translation of Tantia Topi's confession and orders.

[50]See Sen, *1857*, p. 278; for Kunwar Singh, see K.K. Datta, *Biography of Kunwar Singh and Amar Singh* (Patna, 1957); for Awadh, Mukherjee, *Awadh in Revolt*, pp. 129, 168. In other countries too, in situations of popular insurgency, the actions of landed magnates and the gentry have been constrained by popular pressure: see, for example, M. James, 'Obedience and Dissent in Henrician England: The Lincolnshire Rebellion, 1536', in M. James, *Society, Politics and Culture: Studies in Early Modern England* (Cambridge, 1986), pp. 256–57.

and the various regional principalities—not because it was idyllic and less oppressive, but because it was familiar. British conquest and the imposition of British administration and western practices were seen as something grotesque: hostile, alien and inhuman. The familiar world of the people had been turned topsy-turvy and they wanted it restored. Hence the 'natural' affiliation to the representatives of the previous order: in Delhi to the Mughal emperor, in Awadh to the boy-king Birjis Qadr, in Jhansi to the rani and in Kanpur to the head of the Maratha confederacy, Nana Sahib, the heir to the *peshwa*.

One could say following Hegel that in the initial moment of negation the rebel consciousness was seized by the 'fanaticism of destruction'; only by destroying could that consciousness 'possess the feeling of itself as existent'. Yet the actualization of that destruction 'leads at once to some sort of order'. There is a transition from that fleeting moment of destruction to the 'positing of a determinacy'.[51] The harking-back to the old order was the positing of a content. Or to put it another way, that moment of liberation, when the structures of domination had seemed to pass into something akin to *communitas*, *à La* Victor Turner, when there had been a 'direct, immediate and total confrontation of human identities', could not be sustained for long; and there was a return to the domain of structures, to old hierarchies.[52]

The preceding analysis has emphasized the merging of the sepoy element into the common people and the strength of popular insurgency in the making of the rebellion in Kanpur. Yet at this point in the discussion the specific contribution of the sepoy element probably needs to be re-introduced. The sepoys, despite their peasant origins, were in a unique position. Within the domain of popular insurgency of which they were a definite part, they were the only section which had been proximate to state power. As sons of the peasantry they had left the village, seen the world outside the village and now during the revolt had, as it were, brought the world back to the village. This was a rite of passage through which the peasant became initiated into the mysteries of the state: he graduated from the knowledge of mere officialdom to a knowledge

[51]G. W.F. Hegel, *The Philosophy of Right*, trans. T.M. Knox (Oxford, 1967), para. 5.

[52]Victor Turner, *The Ritual Process: Structure and Anti Structure* (Cornell, 1977), ch. 4, *passim*. The quotation is from p. 132.

of the state as the authentic object of hatred.[53] One sees the hatred writ large in the selection of the rebels' targets. Their proximity to state power had, however, a duplex character. It enabled them, on the one hand, to identify the state as the enemy. On the other hand, the same exposure and experience, especially the many battles they had fought on behalf of the British state in India, had made them realize the importance of leadership, discipline and structures of command in the conduct of war. Their return to the rural community as an armed peasantry was thus informed by a new consciousness. The harking-back to traditional leadership could be the product of that consciousness. It is significant that peasants in revolt usually sought legitimacy in colonial India by appointing somebody from among themselves a leader or a king,[54] but in 1857 dethroned kings or dispossessed princes, that is those that had previously established claims to leadership, were chosen to lead and give the uprising a legitimacy. An older and legitimate political order had lost to the British in the late eighteenth and early nineteenth centuries; it was as if the sepoys in their quest for leadership and command were reviving that order and fighting a war on its behalf and in its name.

The desire to reinstate the old order was evident in the establishment of courts of law where justice was meted out according to 'native ideas'; in the prohibition of writing in English; in the revival of old offices; in the reappointment of former officials; in the setting up of a council of war; and in the restoration of old court rituals.[55] This is not to say that the sepoys and the ordinary people had completely surrendered their initiative to the Nana and his men. In the council of war the sepoys were strongly represented: in fact it was Teeka Singh, a former sepoy, who was made a general and

[53]Cf. Antonio Gramsci—'the "people" is aware that it has enemies, but only identifies them empirically as the so-called *signori*. Contained in the concept of signore there is much of the old dislike of country for town. There is also dislike of officialdom—the only form in which the State is perceived. The peasant ... hates the civil servant; he does not hate the State for he does not understand it': Antonio Gramsci, *Selections from the Prison Notebooks*, ed. and trans. Quintin Hoare and Geoffrey Nowell Smith (New York, 1971), p. 272.

[54]Guha, *Elementary Aspects of Peasant Insurgency*, pp. 112–15.

[55]The setting up of courts is described in Williams, 'Review of the Evidence'; the prohibition of English in Shepherd, *Personal Narrative of the Outbreak and Massacre at Cawnpore*, p. 41; for the restoration of former officials and rituals, see Nanak Chand's diary, *passim;* 'Synopsis'. For the council of war, see Lt.-Col. Williams, 'Memorandum', in *Narrative, Kanpur.*

put in charge of operations. Other sepoys took the ranks of major, colonel and so on, making evident their desire to have a hierarchy of command.[56] There were also instances when, despite Nana Sahib's disapproval, the rebels humiliated the wealthy collaborators.[57] Again the Nuneh Nawab recorded that:

> One of the sepoys who had been in the entrenchment [with the British] and was seized and confined on 27 June had a son in the 2nd Light Cavalry, who first went to Baba Bhut and menacing to kill him in case of non-compliance with his request, he was referred to Nana, to whom he went and repeated his request in the same threatening manner. Nana immediately liberated his father and his comrades.[58]

Pushed to an extreme, an ordinary rebel could even breach the codes of deference to a leader, speak threateningly to him and have him overlook such a serious 'crime' as loyalty to the British. The leaders, in their turn, recognizing the strength and importance of the people, sought to keep them happy. Thus we read in Tantia Topi's 'order book' instructions such as 'Anyone who takes wood etc. from the Godown or from the houses of the poor, should be punished by order of a Court'; or again 'all the commanding officers are requested to give strict order to their men ... that if they are found extorting money from the poor villagers or plundering them they will be severely punished'.[59] There is a deliberate coming together here of the two domains, of the popular and that represented by a feudal leader like Nana Sahib and his men. It leads to the formation of a united front against a common enemy whose complete annihilation alone can lead to a stable reconstitution of the old order. Azimullah represented the position:

> What fools, then we natives have made of ourselves, so quietly to surrender our country to a handful of tyrannical foreigners, who are trying in many ways to deprive us of our religion and our privileges! It behoves us, therefore—and I call upon you all to join heart and

[56]'Synopsis'; also Rizvi and Bhargava (eds), *Freedom Struggle*, iv, p. 669.

[57]I.O.L.R., Board's Collection, no. 195724, translation of the diary of the Nuneh Nawab.

[58]Ibid.

[59]I.O.L.R., Home Miscellaneous, no. 727A, translation of Tantia Topi's confession and orders.

> hand—to extirpate our enemies, root and branch, from the face of all India. Let not a soul escape, let not the name of a Christian be ever named in Hindoostan. We are strong and numerous to keep our own.[60]

There is a statement here of unity, strength and confidence; the enemy is clearly identified and annihilation clearly proclaimed as the purpose. *Ishtahars* (proclamations) were issued in both Urdu and in Devnagiri calling upon 'all Hindoos and Mahomedans to unite in defence of their religion and present themselves for service'.[61] A mutiny leading to a collective attack on the dominators had now been transformed into an entire society's war against a common enemy.

An insurrection, by its collective nature, by its acceptance of a leadership and by seeking its identity with a political order, had acquired legitimacy for itself. It was now public and open. Nana Sahib could thus inform General Wheeler in the entrenchment that the attack was going to commence.[62]

From the extant evidence it seems that the massacre on the river was a stratagem in the conduct of the war. It was planned in advance. The idea of luring the British out of the entrenchment and then killing them *en masse* was probably suggested by a statement made by W.J. Shepherd, who had left the entrenchment disguised as a native and had been apprehended. To quote Shepherd,

> a man, having the appearance of one in authority, came to me and asked if I could tell whether the officers and Europeans were anxious to leave the station, and if, in the event of an offer being made to that effect, it would be accepted. I replied that I could not exactly tell, but that the females were certainly anxious to get away by any means, and for their sakes no doubt such an offer would be accepted if made in a satisfactory manner.[63]

Shepherd, needless to add, had no idea of what this statement would lead to; he was trying to free his countrymen, including his family, from the torment that they suffered within the entrenchment.

[60] Shepherd, *Personal Narrative of the Outbreak and Massacre at Cawnpore*, p. 42.

[61] 'Synopsis'.

[62] 'The next day June 7th Gen. Wheeler received a note stating that the Nana intended to attack him': I.O.L.R., Papers of General Sir Mowbray Thomson, Photo Eur 137.

[63] Shepherd, *Personal Narrative of the Outbreak and Massacre at Cawnpore*, p. 69.

A full council met, and decided that the best way to defeat the British was to get them out of the entrenchment with the promise of a safe passage down the river and then kill them. It is significant that this council was attended not only by Nana Sahib, his men like Azimullah and rebels like Teeka Singh, but also by Maulavi Liakat Ali.[64] A Hindu prince and a *maulavi* (muslim religious teacher) sanctioned the massacre. The decision to slaughter in this manner also seemed to have the sanction of the *qazi* (judge): a witness reported

> Two days before the boats for the Europeans were got ready, in the evening the Kazi [Wasiuddin] with two *sirdars* of the cavalry regiment whose names I don't know, was concerting measures at his own house for their death. At that time I arrived at the house and heard that to murder the Europeans having got them out of the entrenchment was *lawful and proper.*'[65]

The massacre could thus take on the nature of an execution, of an open and public affair. It was a spectacle watched by some ten to twelve thousand people.[66] And in the manner of executioners some of the rebels told a group of Englishmen, 'now repent of all your misdeeds and ask pardon of God'.[67]

The public and open character of the massacre on the river is testified by all the eyewitness accounts that there are of the event. At the risk of being gory and prolix I quote from three of these. Here is the massacre as seen by Mowbray Thomson, who escaped on one of the two boats that got away, and swam to the shore and was rescued by a landed magnate:

> Major Vibart and his family were the last to go on board, a party of his Regiment, the 2nd cavalry, escorted him down and insisted on his taking all that belonged to him on board the boats but when they saw him fairly embarked and us trying to get our boats away from the bank, they made signal to the boatmen who immediately left us, having previously set fire into the thatched covering of the boats, which broke out instantly in a blaze. Everyone who could

[64]'Synopsis'.

[65]Deposition of Hulas Singh, in *Depositions at Cawnpore*. Emphasis added.

[66]Deposition of Khuda Bux, ibid. All eyewitnesses confirm that there was a big crowd at the ghat; for example Ganga Singh in his narrative said, 'Indeed, it was difficult to get there, as there was an enormous crowd of Soldiers as well as people of the Town looking on': I.O.L.R., Board's Collection, no. 195718.

[67]Deposition of John Fitchett, in *Depositions at Cawnpore*.

> was obliged to jump over board. The wounded and helpless who could not, perished in the flames. The Cavalry men were first to fire on us and their firing appeared to be the signal for the massacre to commence, for the instant afterwards four guns opened on the forty boats which had [been] provided for us and about 10,000 muskets.[68]

Eliza Bradshaw had an incredible escape. She stood in the water with the blood-bath all around her and succeeded in 'secreting' herself to a Muslim cemetery. She thus lived to describe the scene:

> At sunrise on the 27th, some hackeries, three or four elephants, and three *palkees* [palanquin] were brought into the entrenchments ... The General and some officers were on elephants, Mrs Wheeler was in a *palkee* ... The ladies were on the hackeries ... We were about the centre with the drummers and their families. The sowars and sepoys were on our right and left ... When we reached the bridge with the white railings near Colonel William's house, we saw a large crowd assembled, men from the city and villagers; the sowars who were ahead, shouted out that they were to stand aside, and none to come down to the *ghat*; we then descended into the dry *nullah* [watercourse] leading to the river. When we got to our boat, we found that it had no bamboo flooring ... Suddenly we heard firing, and the pattering of bullets, and then the roar of cannon on both sides of the river. We jumped out, the boat was between us and shore. In the water, a few paces off, by the next boat we saw the Colonel's youngest daughter. A sepoy was going to kill her with his bayonet. She said, 'My father was always kind to sepoys.' He turned away, and just then a villager struck her in the head with a club, and she fell into the water ... we saw the clergyman take out a book, we did not see him read it, for a sowar rode into the water and cut him down with a blow on the neck; he then killed the Padre, and the other, who was a missionary ... A sepoy killed a child with his bayonet ... another sepoy took a young child by the leg and threw it into the water.[69]

Amelia Horne, who was taken away from the site of the massacre by a sepoy as his 'prize', as it were, recalled many years later:

> While we were endeavouring to embark the shore was lined with spectators, who were looking on and exulting like so many demons,

[68]I.O.L.R., Papers of General Sir Mowbray Thomson, Photo Eur 137.
[69]Deposition of Eliza Bradshaw, in *Depositions at Cawnpore*.

> as they undoubtedly were, over our distressing condition, taunting and jeering at us for having at last fallen into their hands. The black devils grinned like so many apes, keeping up an incessant chatter in their monkey language.
>
> After all had embarked—which took about two hours to accomplish—the word was given to proceed. Instead of the crew obeying these orders, a signal was given from the shore and they all leaped into the water and waded to the bank, after having first secreted burning charcoal in the thatch of most of the boats. Immediately a volley of bullets assailed us, followed by a hail of shot and grape which struck the boats ... In a few minutes pandemonium reigned. Several of the boats were seen to be wrapped in flames, and the sick and wounded were burnt to death. Some jumped overboard and tried to swim to the opposite shore, but were picked off by the bullets of the sepoys ... the guns continued their vile work, and grape and musketry were poured ... from the opposite bank which soon became alive with rebels who had been placed there to intercept refugees to that shore. A few succeeded in pushing their boats to the further side of the river and were mercilessly slaughtered. The cavalry waded into the river with drawn swords and cut down those who were still alive ... The water was red with blood and the smoke from the firing of the cannon and muskets and the fire from the burning boats, lay like dense clouds over and around us ... the sepoys laughed and cheered, inciting each other to greater acts of brutality![70]

There was no attempt to conceal the hatred and the violence. The guns and troops were strategically placed to prevent escape. The two boats that did get away were chased and shot down. The rebels took up their positions at night and orders were given to the neighbouring zamindars (land-holders) and villagers to be present at the *ghat*. And they were present, 'armed', one witness reported, 'with swords, and battle axes'.[71] Things were so arranged as to overpower the British: according to Shepherd, 'The English were entirely in their power'.[72] The massacre was also executed in keeping with a very definite plan. The boatmen set fire to the thatched awnings at a signal, and the guns opened fire at the sound of a bugle. The rebels on horseback went into the water to slash the survivors on very definite orders from Tantia Topi. The operations were supervised

[70]Brit. Lib., Papers relating to the Indian Mutiny, i, Amy Haines's Narrative.

[71]Deposition of Peer Bux, in *Depositions at Cawnpore.*

[72]Shepherd, *Personal Narrative of the Outbreak and Massacre at Cawnpore*, p. 73.

by Teeka Singh, Jwala Prasad (an associate of Nana Sahib who had been given the rank of brigadier), a cavalry trooper called Nukkee, and Tantia Topi, all of whom sat on a specially built platform.[73] Everybody present was implicated in the violence, either directly or as a part of a crowd that watched and exulted. The massacre was a collective affair: an expression of an entire society's hatred and rejection of an alien order. It was a spectacle of rebel power.

The massacre could thus be celebrated as a great victory. Gun salutes were fired to mark the occasion. Nana Sahib took his seat on a throne and the sacred mark was put on his forehead. The city was illuminated for the victory.[74] In the surrounding villages too there was a certain atmosphere, for, Nanak Chand recorded, 'The daring speeches of the villagers frightened me out of my wits'.'[75] A proclamation announced the victory and the establishment of a new power:

> As by the bounty of the glorious Almighty and the enemy-destroying fortune of the Emperor the yellow-faced and narrow-minded people have been sent to hell, and Cawnpore has been conquered, it is necessary that all the subjects and landowners should be as obedient to the present Government as they have been to the former one; that all the Government servants should promptly and cheerfully engage their whole mind in executing the orders of the Government; that it is the incumbent duty of all the peasants and landed proprietors of every district to rejoice at the thought that the Christians have been sent to hell, and both the Hindoo and Mahomedan religions have been confirmed; and that they should as usual be obedient to the authorities of the Government, and never suffer any complaint against themselves to reach to the ears of the higher authority.[76]

The affirmation of rebel power with such brutality and violence also has another context related to British counter-insurgency measures. As the British administration in Calcutta recovered from the shock of the uprising they took immediate measures to quell it. The forces sent up to north India under Neill and Havelock had

[73]These details are stated in the depositions of Goordial, Lochun, Nundeedeen Aheer, Jagganath and Peer Bux, in *Depositions at Cawnpore.*

[74]'Synopsis'.

[75]Nanak Chand's diary: 27 June 1857.

[76]Quoted in Trevelyan, *Cawnpore*, p. 141.

three aims: the re-establishment of British authority; punishing the rebels; and relieving the British garrisons in Kanpur and Lucknow. Neill arrived in Allahabad on 11 June; this was to serve as his first base for the taking of Kanpur. But before he could move to Kanpur, he had to 'settle' the town of Allahabad and its surrounding countryside. His methods were simple. He ordered his troops to go into towns and villages and to kill and burn indiscriminately; old men, women and children were not spared. Here is Kaye, a writer not known for being sympathetic to the revolt, writing about Neill's operations:

> Over the whole of the Sepoy War—there is no darker cloud than that which gathered over Allahabad in this terrible summer ... It is on the records of our British Parliament, in papers sent home by the Governor-General of India in Council, that 'the aged, women and children, are sacrificed, as well as those guilty of rebellion.' They were not deliberately hanged, but burnt to death in their villages ... Englishmen did not hesitate to boast, or to record their boastings in writing, that they had 'spared no one' and that 'peppering away at niggers' was very pleasant pastime.[77]

William Howard Russell was in India in 1858, and he met an officer who was a part of the column that moved up from Allahabad towards Kanpur. The officer reported, in Russell's words, that 'In two days forty-two men were hanged on the roadside, and a batch of twelve men were executed because their faces were 'turned the wrong way' when they were met on the march. All the villages in his front were burned'.[78] Even boys who had playfully flaunted rebel colours and beaten a tom-tom were killed.[79]

The motives for such butchery were also clear. The British were unable to accept that a subject population had taken arms against them, had dared to destroy their property and lives. As Kaye put it,

[77]Kaye, *History of the Sepoy War, 1857–58*, ii, pp. 269–70. Neill's orders, according to Kaye (p. 275), were that 'all the men inhabiting them [certain villages, previously marked out] were to be slaughtered. All sepoys of mutinous regiments not giving a good account of themselves were to be hanged. The town of Futtehpore which had revolted was to be attacked, and the Pathan quarters destroyed, with all their inhabitants. All heads of insurgents, particularly at Futtehpore, to be hanged. If the Deputy Collector is taken, hang him, and have his head cut off and stuck up on one of the principal (Mahomedan) buildings of the town'.

[78]Russell, *My Indian Mutiny Diary*, pp. 281–82.

[79]Narrated in E. Thompson, *The Other Side of the Medal* (New York, 1926), p. 72.

> So it happened that whilst the first bitterness of our degradation—*the degradation of fearing those whom we had taught to fear us*—was still fresh upon our people, there came a sudden accession of stout English hearts and strong English hands, ready at once to punish and to awe.[80]

John Lawrence, the governor of the Punjab and a very influential administrator, laid down the priorities of British policy: 'Our object is to make an example and terrify others'.[81]

What is significant is that these killings by the British troops were carried out before the massacre in Kanpur.[82] It is not far-fetched to imagine that the news of such massacres reached the rebel stronghold. They wanted to counter this show of violence by their own exhibition of power. They 'borrowed' from the British and replicated the violence. The terms of their violence were thus derived from that very structure of power against which they had revolted.[83]

But was it merely 'borrowing'? Or are we being too hasty in pointing to the derivative character of the rebels' use of violence? Is there not something more significant in this tremendous display of force and power? Rebel power, in however tentative a fashion, constituted itself as an alternative order; as a sovereign power that sought its identity in the pre-British eighteenth-century political system. The British presence was, therefore, an obstacle to the reconstitution of that sovereignty. The massacre restored the sovereignty by manifesting it at its most spectacular. By a display of terror not dissimilar to the terror the British deployed, it sought to create an awareness of its unrestrained and independent presence. The spectacle reactivated the power that British rule had undermined. This was a power that embarked on its career, as indeed rebel power always does, not by trying to enforce its laws but by clearly marking out its enemy.

The intensity and ferocity of the violence was also related to the imbrication of the revolt with profound religious feelings. As Natalie Zemon Davis has noted, 'religious violence is intense because it

[80]Kaye, *History of the Sepoy War*, ii, p. 269. Emphasis added.

[81]Quoted in Thompson, *Other Side of the Medal*, p. 40.

[82]'These "severities" could not have been justified by the Cawnpore massacre, because they took place before that diabolical act': Russell, *My Indian Mutiny Diary*, p. 282.

[83]Guha, *Elementary Aspects of Peasant Insurgency*, p. 75.

connects intimately with the fundamental values and self-definition of a community'. Like the crowds of late sixteenth-century France, the rebels in Kanpur had a sense that what they were doing was legitimate; they fought and destroyed in defence of their religion, and their violence had a structure—dramatic and spectacular. What was seen as grotesque was destroyed in a grotesque way, by dehumanizing the victims.[84] British rule, as I have emphasized, inscribed its domination on the body of the Indian. To eradicate the marks of that domination, a rebel power had to, in its turn, destroy the body of the Briton. The violence embedded in British rule was eradicated through counter-violence: British power had to be disembodied for the rebel power to be completely sovereign. 'The very excess of the violence employed' in the massacre, one could say following Foucault, was 'one of the elements of its glory'.[85]

The glory was all the greater because the massacre was seen by the rebels as divine retribution. The English officer who collected the evidence on the massacre remarked in his synopsis that this was a period 'when Satan may truly be said to have been let loose upon earth'.[86] A group of captured sepoys, minutes before their execution, were asked individually why they had killed their British masters; each one of them replied that 'the slaughter of the British was required by our religion'.[87] What was the work of God for one was the work of Satan for the other. In that abstract contraposition is perhaps captured the configuration of two contesting systems of power. The massacre at Satichaura Ghat on 27 June 1857 was a dramatic moment when a body politic struggled to recover its totality by destroying the body of its dominant other.

The narrative of violence in Kanpur does not end here. The massacre on the river was followed by a second massacre, the nature of which was distinct from that of the first. This involved those who had survived the slaughter at Satichaura Ghat. The men were separated out from the survivors and shot. It was a straight shooting,

[84]Natalie Zemon Davis, 'The Rites of Violence', in N. Z. Davis, *Society and Culture in Early Modern France* (Oxford, 1987 edn.), pp. 181, 186–87, *passim.*

[85]The above paragraph is based on my reading of M. Foucault, *Discipline and Punish: The Birth of the Prison* (Harmondsworth, 1979), esp. ch. 2; Guha, *Elementary Aspects of Peasant Insurgency*, pp. 164–6. The quotation is from p. 32 of *Discipline and Punish.*

[86]'Synopsis'.

[87]Ball, *History of the Indian Mutiny*, ii, p. 242.

as if in continuation of what had happened on the river. The women and children were kept as prisoners in a room, known as the Bibighur.

In the meantime, in the rebel camp, preparations had to be made to stop the British forces marching up from Allahabad. The rebel forces were defeated in two hard-fought encounters on 15 July, in the village of Aong and on the banks of Pandu Nadi. The rebels now retreated to Kanpur, facing the prospect of a British take-over of the city. It was then decided that the ladies and children were to be killed. A personal servant of Nana Sahib, named Begum, who was in charge of the prisoners, brought orders from the Nana for the sepoys to kill the women and children. The sepoys refused to comply, and fired a few volleys aimed at the ceiling. At this four or five professional executioners were sent in armed with swords and long knives, and they cut up the prisoners. The bodies—it was said that not all were dead—were thrown into a well.[88]

In this episode there is clear evidence that the unity that had previously been forged began to break down with the advance of the British forces and the defeats suffered by the rebels. The rebels clearly refused to obey their leader. Defeat had led to a loss of legitimacy. The leaders now had to fall back upon their personal servants and on mercenaries. The men who were called in to carry out the killing were paid.[89] This massacre, unlike the first one, was no longer an open affair. It was carried out in a closed room. The people around could not see the killing. The massacre no longer had the sanction and participation of an entire society which saw itself as defeated. Lieutenant-Colonel Williams indicated this when he commented in his synopsis of the evidence:

> Regarding the numerous massacres that took place, the evidence ... is clearly and freely given, but on approaching the last and most terrible scene, all seem instinctively to shrink from confessing any knowledge of so foul and barbarous a crime as the indiscriminate slaughter of helpless women and innocent children. Evidence that runs clear and strong from 15th of May to 14th of July, suddenly ceases on the fatal day of the 15th of that month.[90]

The very way in which the massacre was carried out eliminated the possibility of any direct witnesses, since it was in a closed room.

[88]'Synopsis'.
[89]Ibid.
[90]Ibid.

There were people outside, but they, as Williams noted, refused to speak about what they had seen or heard. Do we detect in this silence, this reticence, disapproval? People had exulted in the first massacre; they disowned the second by remaining silent. Sepoys who had killed on the river were unwilling to obey orders. Thus the first was a spectacle, the other carried out indoors; one had been a show of power, the other an act of retreat. The second massacre was the work of a leadership no longer sure of its power, its mass support, and therefore of its victory. The leadership wanted to kill because it wanted to remove witnesses of its own complicity. It was a massacre produced by fear. The massacre of Satichaura and the massacre at Bibighur were based on two different codes of violence. Contrasting crime with insurgency, a historian of peasant insurgency in colonial India writes that 'the criminal may be said to stand in the same relation to the insurgent as does what is conspiratorial (or secretive) to what is public (or open), or what is individualistic (or small group) to what is communal (or mass) in character'.[91] It was indeed an irony that under pressure from British counter-insurgency measures, in the space of a fortnight the power of the insurrection had transformed itself from the public to the secretive: from the communal to only the leadership: what had previously been seen as a work of God had become, one could say using the same terms, an act of Satan.

A POSTSCRIPT ON RAPE

It would have been convenient if one could leave the analysis of rebel violence and its nature at this point. To do so would be to leave the narrative without observing a significant absence. Here was a society in open war with a foreign power; at the time when the rebels seemed to be victorious they had British women at their mercy for about fifteen days. Yet there was no rape. Williams concluded after his investigations that 'the most searching and earnest enquiries totally disprove the unfounded assertion that was at first so frequently made, and so currently believed, that personal indignity and dishonour had been offered to our poor suffering country women'.[92] Witnesses who had been very close to where the ladies had been imprisoned testified that nobody had molested

[91]Guha, *Elementary Aspects of Peasant Insurgency*, p. 79.
[92]'Synopsis'.

the women.[93] In 1858 Lord Canning ordered a full inquiry on the dishonouring of British women by the rebels all over north India. The findings of the inquiry were very definite:

> ... nothing has come to my knowledge which would in the smallest degree support any of the tales of dishonour current in our public prints. Direct evidence, wherever procurable, has been steadily and consistent against them. The people, those who must know had there been cases of outraged honour and would have told us, uniformly deny that such things were ever perpetrated or thought of.[94]

Officer after officer from the districts wrote to say that they had found no evidence of dishonour to women.[95]

What are we to make of this absence? I would like to suggest two possible explanations. The revolt of 1857 visualized itself as a war of religion, a struggle to preserve the purity of caste and religion against a perceived attempt at contamination by the British. The maintenance of purity went so far as to label all loyalists as Christians.[96] It was said that in conversation among the rebels the British were never mentioned for 'a man's mouth became impure [for] forty days by naming the Kafirs'.[97] In such a situation contact of any kind with British women would obviously be considered polluting. The preservation of religious and caste purity could thus eliminate rape.

The aim of the rebels, as I have tried to emphasize, was the destruction of all things British. As Muir, who conducted the enquiry ordered by Lord Canning put it, 'the object of the mutineers was ... not so much to disgrace our name, as to wipe out all traces of Europeans, and of everything connected with foreign rule'.[98] Rape was probably seen as an instrument of defilement, a method of

[93]Depositions of William Clarke, Eliza Bradshaw and Hingun, in *Depositions at Cawnpore.*

[94]I.O.L.R., Home Miscellaneous, no. 725, 'Memorandum containing the Result of Enquiries made by Desire of the Governor General into the Rumours of European Females having been Dishonoured during the Late Mutinies'.

[95]Ibid., enclosures.

[96]Deposition of Khoda Bux, in *Depositions at Cawnpore.*

[97]Deposition of John Fitchett, ibid.

[98]I.O.L.R., Home Miscellaneous, no. 725, 'Memorandum containing the Result of Enquiries made by Desire of the Governor General into the Rumours of European Females having been Dishonoured during the Late Mutinies'.

subordination which polluted the blood and body of women by the most intimate and forceful contact. This was not the agenda of the rebels. They were driven by the idea of annihilating the British; this is how they wanted to show and establish their power. That power did not distinguish by way of gender or age. In that context when the desire to destroy was overwhelming, rape became redundant.

GROUP OF SEPOYS AT LUCKNOW.—FROM A PHOTOGRAPH.

The Sepoys of the Bengal Army
Courtesy: *Wiki Commons*

The sepoys of the Bengal Army who were the first to raise the flag of revolt across the many garrisons spread over North India came from peasant backgrounds. They were mostly from southern districts of Awadh and were Brahmins. The discipline of the British Indian army made the peasants into sepoys but this process could not eradicate the links the sepoys had with their rural background. When their *dharma* and *deen* were threatened by a slew of British policies, they turned against their masters and killed them irrespective of gender and age.

The Sipahi and the Sepoy Mutinies

The revolt of 1857 or the Indian Mutiny, as it is still conveniently labelled in most of the western world, was spread over a large area covering from Delhi in the north-west to Bihar in the east, and from the foothills of the Himalayas to Jhansi. There were scattered instances of revolt outside this area. Within the area, again, the region north of the river Yamuna right upto Awadh seems to have been the core where the sepoy mutinies were clustered and the rebellion most popular and intense.

This paper concentrates, against the current fashion, on the sepoy mutinies: on the *sipahi* and his activities. There are reasons for looking at the sepoy mutinies separately. In the literature on 1857, rich as it is, this is a neglected aspect. In the nineteenth-century, in the high noon of British imperialism, when the great narratives of the 'Mutiny' were written, the activities of the sepoys were written about as something disorderly and chaotic: the work of disloyal soldiery. This could give rise to ambiguities. For example, J.W. Kaye called his account, *The History of the Sepoy War, 1857–58*. For him, the events of 1857 were nothing more than the work of sepoys, a very small section of the population; yet, he called it a 'war' a term that implies the involvement of a large section of the population and also more importantly, a degree of planning, co-ordination and organization. More recently, Eric Stokes has drawn attention to the military tactics of the sepoys.[1] But, for him, the

This essay first appeared in M. Hassan and N. Gupta (eds) *India's Colonial Encounter: Essays in Memory of Eric Stokes* (Delhi, 1993).

[1]Eric Stokes, *The Peasant Armed: The Indian Revolt of 1857*, edited by C.A. Bayly (Oxford, 1986). Ch. 2.

mutinies were 'the work of a small minority'; the mutinies were the product of 'designing men'; a conspiring few substituted for collective action.[2] In nationalist historiography, prone as it is to prove that 1857 was much more than a mutiny, the tendency is to gloss over the activities of the sepoy. Thus, in the writings of S.B. Chaudhuri, the activities of the sepoys are not discussed; he writes only about the civil rebellions which, to him, were important.[3] This paper will attempt to show that these approaches are flawed: they fundamentally misunderstand the nature of sepoy action, thereby also missing the crucial interconnections between the sepoy mutinies and the popular rebellion.

I have argued elsewhere[4] that a chronological survey of the mutinies suggests a certain pattern. The first outbreak takes place on 10 May at Meerut. There the soldiers having mutinied sped off towards Delhi. It is significant that between 10 and 14 May there were no mutinies in any of the garrisons of north India. It is only after the sepoys in Delhi had mutinied (11–12 May) that the other garrisons in north India follow suit as if in chain reaction: 20 May-Aligarh, 23 May-Etwah, and Mainpuri, 27 May-Etah, 30 May-Lucknow, 4 June-Kanpur and so on. There is here a contagion of movement facilitated by the fact that there was a degree of communication between the sepoy lines. Often, such communication could be direct. The 7th Awadh Irregular Infantry, who had refused to take the cartridges in early May, wrote to the 48th Native Infantry that 'they had acted for the faith and awaited the 48th orders'.[5] Men moved from one cantonment to another carrying the message of mutiny: in Kaye's words these were the 'emissaries of evil'.[6] Sepoys came from Benaras to Lucknow, British officers reported, 'to corrupt the troops'.[7] The sepoy lines in Fyzabad

[2]Ibid., pp. 50 and 54.

[3]S.B. Chaudhuri, *Civil Rebellion in the Indian Mutinies, 1857–59* (Calcutta, 1957).

[4]R. Mukherjee, *Awadh in Revolt, 1857–58: A Study of Popular Resistance* (Delhi, 1984), p. 65.

[5]National Archives of India (NAI): Foreign Dept., Secret Consultations, 18, Dec., 1857, no. 565: Henry Lawrence to Canning, 3 May 1857.

[6]J.W. Kaye, *History of the Sepoy War, 1857–58*, 3 vols (London, 1880; Reprint, New Delhi, 1988), ii, p. 244.

[7]S.A. Rizvi and M.L. Bhargava (eds), *Freedom Struggle in Uttar Pradesh*, 6 vols (Lucknow, 1957), ii, p. 14.

were swarming with mutinous sepoys from neighbouring Azamgarh and Jaunpur.[8] In Salon, the mutiny occurred only when mutineers from Allahabad, Sultanpur and Partapgarh had come there and 'goaded' the troops in Salon to rise.[9]

Edwards, the Magistrate of Budaun, noted that the 10th N.I. in Fatehgarh would mutiny depending on the movements of other mutinous corps with whom they were in daily correspondence.[10] In the context of communication of the message of revolt, the experience of Francois Sisten, a native Christian police inspector in Sitapur, is revealing. He had gone to pay his respects to the joint magistrate of Saharanpur and was dressed and seated like an Indian. A Muslim *tahsildar* of Bijnor entered and asked Sisten where he was from. On hearing that the latter was from Awadh, the *tahsildar* said, 'What news from Awadh? How does the work progress, brother?' Sisten replied, 'If we have work in Awadh your highness will know it well.' The *tahsildar* interpreting this as caution said: 'Depend upon it, we will succeed this time, the direction of the business is in able hands.' People were thus planning and talking of the uprising. In fact, the *tahsildar* was later to be the chief rebel leader of Bijnor.[11]

There were other instances, too, of communication through nonmilitary sources. The official narrative for Meerut noted that

> one of the many emissaries who were moving about the country, appeared at Meerut in April, ostensibly as a fukeer, riding on an elephant with the follower and having with him horses and native carriages. The frequent visits of the men of the native regiments to him attracted attention and he was ordered through the police to leave the place. He apparently complied, but it is said, he stayed some time in the lines of the 20th N.I.[12]

[8]NAI: For. Dept., Secret Cons., 25 Sept. 1857, Cons. No 398: E.O. Bradford to Edmonstone, 2 July 1857.

[9]Barrow's narrative in G. Hutchinson, *Narrative of the Mutinies in Oude* (London, 1859), pp. 127ff.

[10]W. Edwards, *Personal Adventures during the Indian Rebellion in Rohilcund, Futtehghur and Oude* (1858; Reprint Allahabad, 1974), p. 65.

[11]R.H. W. Dunlop, *Service and Adventure with the khakee ressalah or Meerut Volunteer Force, during the Mutinies of 1857–1858*; (1858; Reprint Allahabad, 1974), pp. 153–54.

[12]*Narratives of Events attending the outbreak of disturbances and the Restoration of Authority* (Calcutta, 1858), Meerut, p. 250. para 152.

Lucknow, too, immediately after the annexation of Awadh, was full of religious leaders and self-styled prophets all preaching the destruction of British rule.[13] The outbreak of the mutinies was not chaotic or disorderly. On the contrary, the *sipahis* showed a remarkable degree of planning and co-ordination in the way the mutinies were carried out. The mutinies began at a pre-appointed signal: in Bareilly, Lucknow and Meerut the signal was the firing of the evening gun. In Fyzahad it was the sounding of the bugle at 10.00 p.m.[14] In Kanpur, the sounding of the bugle was the signal for the massacre to begin at Satichaupura Ghat.[15] The execution of the mutiny, in most places, was well-planned. In Fyzabad, for example, as the bugle sounded the troops quickly organized themselves: they stopped the gunners from touching their guns and under the direction of a *risaldar* (an Indian infantry officer) the English officers of the 22nd and 6th were placed with the Quarter Guard. The *sawars* patrolled all roads and approaches to the cantonment.[16]

Such instances indicate planning and suggest a decision-making body which laid down the plan of action. The crucial question is, of course, what were such bodies, and how and when they were formed. Unfortunately, no direct answers to these questions can be provided. But from two events one can get clues as to how the mutinies came to be so well-organized. The first is the experience of Captain Hearsey of the Awadh Military Police. During the mutiny he had been given protection by his Indian subordinates. The 41st Native Infantry, stationed in the same place, insisted that as they had murdered all their officers it was necessary for the military police to do the same or deliver Hearsey up as prisoner to the 41st. The Military Police refused to do either and so it was decided to settle the matter by referring it to a *panchayat*, i.e., a collective body composed of native officers drawn from each regiment.[17] Ball in his *The History of the Indian Mutiny* noted that *panchayats* were a nightly occurrence in the

[13]Mukherjee, *Awadh in Revolt*, pp. 36–37.

[14]Ibid., p. 68 and note 19.

[15]The massacre at Satichaura Ghat is analysed and reconstructed in R. Mukherjee, '"Satan Let Loose Upon Earth": The Massacres in Kanpur in the Revolt of 1857', in *Past and Present* (August 1990).

[16]Mukherjee, *Awadh in Revolt*, p. 70.

[17]Hearsey's narrative in Hutchinson, *Narrative*, p. 97.

Kanpur sepoy lines.[18] There is a suggestion here that matters were decided collectively and given the character of the sepoy lines it is not difficult to imagine sepoys sitting together to decide their own future.

The other piece of evidence is a little more vivid. It concerns the Mangal Pandey episode. This is one of the better documented episodes of the Revolt and its origins. The investigations revealed that before Mangal Pandey decided to act there had been midnight meetings in Barrackpore which had been attended by sepoys from different regiments. And, on that fateful afternoon when he opened fire on his officers none except one of his fellow sepoys, all of whom had gathered around, tried to stop him. The only exception was Sheikh Paltu. In fact the other sepoys displayed a complicity, for while Mangal Pandey drew his sword and slashed and wounded Lieutenant Baugh, an unidentified sepoy hit Sgt.-Major Hewson from behind. During his trial, Mangal Pandey steadfastly refused, in a remarkable show of solidarity, to name the sepoys who were implicated. He had only one answer that he had acted on his own. His reiteration of his own responsibility for his own actions can be read as an attempt to shield the reality which was the exact opposite of an individual acting on his own. The collective aspect was again made evident when sepoys of the 34th, Mangal Pandey's regiment trampled their caps on the ground when they were disarmed. A gesture of protest carried out collectively which would in a month's time transform itself to more violent and concrete forms.[19]

The sepoys were thus the makers of their own rebellion: they did not undertake to challenge the might of the Company Bahadur in a fit of absent-mindedness. They were conscious agents and their acts were marked by deliberation and planning. This needs emphasis because all too often in the literature on the subject their actions are described as 'spontaneous', i.e., lacking a coherent programme and plan. As Gramsci wrote, it is only a 'scholastic and academic historico-political outlook which sees as real and worthwhile only such movements of revolt as are one hundred per

[18] C. Ball, *The History of the Indian Mutiny*, 2 vols (London, n.d.), pp. 299–300.

[19] The evidence for this paragraph is taken from C. Hibbert, *The Great Mutiny: India 1857* (Harmondsworth, 1978), pp. 65, 69, 70 and 72. In reconstructing the episode Hibbert draws on G.W. Forrest, *Selections from Letters, Despatches and State Papers in the Military Department of the Govt. of India 1857–58*, 4 vols (Calcutta, 1893–1912).

cent conscious, i.e., movements that are governed by plans worked out in advance to the last detail or in line with abstract theory.' Indeed, as Gramsci would have it, 'pure' spontaneity does not exist in history.' The sepoys had a consciousness which was framed, one could say following Gramsci, 'through everyday experience illuminated by "common sense"'.[20] As conscious agents the sepoys chose to destroy. Direct action, that commonest form of popular protest, informed the sepoys' moment of insurgency. In each and every station the commencement of the mutiny was marked by extensive arson and plunder. The official narrative from Meerut described the ferocity of the destruction, the inveterate animosity with which the work of destruction was carried out ... may be judged of by the fact, that houses built entirely of masonary, with nothing inflammable, except the doors and beams which a considerable height from the ground supported the roof formed of cement, resting on kiln-burnt bricks, were as effectually destroyed as the thatched bungalows. Property, which the miscreants could not carry off, was thrown out and smashed into fragments, evidently pounded to pieces with heavy clubs.[21]

The mutinies were signalled by arson. Kaye noted this:

> What meetings and conspiracies and oath-takings there may have been in the sipahi's quarter...can only be conjectured; but one form of expression in which the feelings declared themselves, was patent to all. It was written in characters of fire and blazed out of the darkness of the night. From the verandahs of their houses the European officers saw these significant illuminations and knew what they portended.[22]

As W.H. Carey put it, 'And thus the Fire King began to demonstrate an inkling of what was in store for almost every station in the North-Western Provinces.'[23]

The destruction was not indiscriminate. Property owned, used or lived by the British were always the first to be attacked. Thus

[20]See Antonio Gramsci, *Selections from the Prison Notebooks*, edited and translated by Quintin Hoare and Geoffrey Nowell Smith (New York, 1971), pp. 196–200.

[21]*Narrative of Events*, Meerut, *op. cit.*, p. 253, para 192.

[22]Kaye, *Sepoy War*, ii, p. 46.

[23]W.H. Carey, *The Mohammedan Rebellion* (Roorkee, 1857), p. 9: quoted in R. Guha, *Elementary Aspects of Peasant Insurgency in Colonial India* (Delhi, 1983), p. 141.

the bungalows in which the Europeans lived, alien to any kind of Indian residence, were always the first to be attacked and burnt. Buildings identified with the British, their institutions, the symbols of their power were invariably destroyed. Thus, in Aligarh one large indigo factory, the property of an European, went up in flames. Similarly, 'the records of the Suddur Cutcherry and those of four out of eight Tehseels were destroyed.'[24] Invariably, the government offices were the object of rebel wrath. In Etawah, the *kachahri*, the sessions court house, the post office—all symbols of alien domination—were victims of incendiary attacks.[25] Almost always the records of the tahsil were destroyed in a symbolic rejection of all that a foreign power had enshrined in its records. For the rebel the mark of enmity was unmistakable. The enmity could also be extended through association. Friends of the British became enemies of the sepoys. Thus, the Bengalis who were seen as the next thing to a Christian, were plundered and forced to swear allegiance to the 'native' government. Bholanath Chunder, a Bengali, wrote,

> The Bengalis cowered in fear, and awaited within closed doors to have their throats cut. The women raised a dolorous cry at the near prospect of death from massacring their officers, and plundering the Treasury, and letting open the gaol-bird, the sipahis spread through the town to loot the inhabitants. Our friend, as well as his other neighbours were soon eased of all their valuables, but were spared their lives on promise of allegiance to their (the Native) Government.[26]

To most north Indians Bengalis at this time were an object of ridicule; as one of them put it, the Bengalis were only good for being attorneys or for teaching Milton and Shakespeare.[27]

By this logic of extension those that had gained from British rule became targets of rebel fury. Dunlop described vividly one such attack:

> ... many of the prisoners released had enemies in the district, mostly Bunyahs who had brought suits in our courts and the arrival of a period of anarchy was at once seized on by them to wreak a

[24]*Narrative of Events*, Aligarh, p. 217, paras 36 and 37.
[25]R. Guha, *Elementary Aspects*, p. 141.
[26]Quoted in Kaye, *Sepoy War 1857–58*, ii, p. 258.
[27]S.N. Sen, *1857* (Delhi, 1957), p. 29.

> summary revenge on almost all the Bunyah caste. Thus at the village of Bhojpore, the best house, a large brick building with a courtyard in the centre and massive wooden portals, belonged to the family of a Mahajun or Bunyah, by name Beharee Lall, who was a four Biswa (or one fifth) sharer of that village; one of the other shareholders, a Jat, was at the time of the outbreak in prison, confined for debt under the Civil court decree at the suit of the Bunyah. He arrived during the light of the 11th at Bhojpore with a few of his fellow prisoners and at daylight the villagers were collected for an attack on the Bunyah house.[28]

What began as an individual vendetta soon transformed itself into an entire village's fury against an oppressor and led to the latter's destruction.

As the above quotations make evident, one of the obvious targets of destruction was the jail. One of the first things the mutineers did was to break open the jails. It appeared to them to be the epitome of domination of an alien legal system. In Meerut, the mutineers rushed to the new jail, 'dug out of the wall the gratings of some of the windows of the ward ... and took their comrades away' and in the jail 'about 300 or 400 sipahees released the convicts.'[29]

Through the previous one hundred years of colonial rule the sepoys had been kicked, flogged and brutalized: they had seen comrades blown from the mouth of canons. In their own movements against their quondam masters they replicated that violence on the master's property and on the master's body. 'Troopers and sipahees' the official narrative of the Meerut outbreak noted, 'were plundering, burning and destroying in every direction and savagely hunting to death every European, every Christian, man, woman or child they could find.'[30] Such replication is, of course, not uncommon. George Rude in his study of the eighteenth-century crowd in Paris and London wrote, 'The eighteenth-century crowd...could hardly fail to be corrupted by the example set them by their social betters. It was an era of brutal floggings, torture of prisoners and public executions.'[31] Again, Richard Cobb in his study of French popular

[28]Dunlop, *Service and Adventure ... during the Mutinies of 1857–58*, p. 36.

[29]*Narrative of Events*, Meerut, p. 251, para 169; p. 252 para 171.

[30]Ibid., p. 252, para 172.

[31]G. Rude, *Paris and London in the 18th Century* (Reprint: London, 1974), p. 26.

protest juxtaposed the violence of the *sans cullottes* with the violence of the ruling class of the *ancien regime.*[32]

The springboard of this violence was the common hatred of all things British. But this hatred, itself, grew from or was aggravated by two interrelated factors. I have discussed already the contagion of the mutiny in its spread from one sepoy line to another. A similar transmission was noticeable in the rumours that circulated in north India in the summer of 1857. There were rumours about greased cartridges, about flours polluted by the bone-dust of cows and pigs, about the intentions of the British to disarm the sepoys, about forcible conversions to Christianity and about the inevitable end of British rule at the centenary of Plassey.[33] All these rumours circulating at the same time aggregated into one gigantic rumour. Untraceable in their origin and unverifiable in their import, the rumours moved in a powerful current touching on issues that were profoundly close to indigenous sentiments. Like the great fear of 1789 in rural France which Lefebvre analysed, there spread in north India the alarm of a deliberate British plot to despoil the religion of Hindus and Muslims. One British officer stationed in Awadh wrote graphically about it:

> Government it was said had sent up cartloads and boatloads of bone-dust, which was to be mixed with the flour and sweetmeats sold in the bazaar, whereby the whole population would lose their caste. The public mind became greatly excited. On one day, at Sultanpur. It was spread over the station that a boat had reached a certain ghaut on the river Gomtee laden with bone-dust, and the sepoys were hardly restrained from outbreak. A few days later, at the station of Salone, two camels, laden with ammunition, arrived at the house of Captain Thompson, the commandant. It was rumoured that the packages contained bone-dust and a panic spread through station. Not only the sepoys in their lines, but the domestic servants about their officers' bungalows, and the villagers and zemindars attending court, hastily flung away, untasted, the food which they had cooked and fasted for the day. At Lucknow, the rumours which were whispered about were perpetual, and the

[32]R. Cobb, *The Police and the People: French Popular Protest 1789–1820* (Oxford, 1972), pp. 88–89.

[33]For rumours see Mukherjee, *Awadh in Revolt*, pp. 72–76; for a general discussion on rumours in peasant insurgency see Guha, *Elementary Aspects*, pp. 251–77.

> public mind was never allowed to rest. Now it was at one shop, the next day in another bazaar, that despatches of bonedust had, it was asserted, been received. It was in vain that facts were opposed to this prevailing panic.[34]

The people were convinced that there was a move afoot to destroy their caste and religion. The programme of reform and westernization so eagerly pursued and propagated by a generation of British administrators only fuelled such a belief. Rumours brought men together, stoked their suspicions and engendered a common hatred and thereby led to common action.

There was one theme in all these rumours: a threat to religion. The sepoys saw their action as being in defence of their religion. In Meerut, 'small parties of cavalry troopers with cries of 'Yah Ullah' and 'Deen Deen' rushed into the city and called upon the people to join in a religious war against the infidels.'[35] A group of sepoys captured in 1858 were individually asked before the execution why they had taken to arms, each one of them individually replied, 'The slaughter of the English was required by our religion.'[36] In this context, the experiences of Ranjit Singh Bissein, a former *havaldar* of the 63rd N.I. is of some relevance. He was coming into Lucknow on 24 May when he passed a police outpost,

> ... the police [Ranjit Singh reported] ... were lounging on the charpoys. They called him to come and sit down and talk. They said they were new levies stationed there. He asked what duty was assigned to them. They said that they were to oppose any of the Sepoys ... and fight them. But they added, we shall not fight them. Kala kala admee sab eyk hyn. Deen kee bat hyn. Hum log kahi ko beydhuram ho.' All black men are one. It is a matter of religion. Why should we lose our religion.)[37]

Religion served as the source of solidarity and fraternity. Religion for them was something that was imbricated with their entire life: it informed their world-view, it was their fountain of knowledge, it

[34]M. Gubbins, *An Account of the Mutinies in Oude and the Siege of the Lucknow Residency* (London, 1858), p. 86.

[35]*Narrative of Events*, Meerut, p. 251, para 170.

[36]Ball, *History of the Indian Mutiny*, ii, p. 242.

[37]NAI: For Dept., Secret Consultations, 26 June 1857, nos 52–4: Gubbins to Couper, 27 May 1857.

provided them with a practical code of ethics: it was, one could say, following Marx their *point d' honneur.*[38] British rule was seen as a challenge to an entire way of life. Thus the division of sepoys into Hindus and Muslims did not serve, contrary to British expectations, to disunite the rebels. In Lucknow. the sepoys could hail Birjis Qadr as their Krishna.[39] The British, and Christianity, by extension, were identified as the common threat to a cherished and familiar way of life. In Sitapur, the name of the Commissioner, Mr. Christian, became identified with the religion, increasing the wrath and fury of the rebels.[40]

I have been trying so far to draw out some of the general characteristics that informed the actions of the sepoys. These are briefly, collectivity as revealed in the planning and co-ordination, a destruction that discriminated and extended itself by the logic of association, a violence whose chief modality was arson and direct actions which were spurred on by rumours. In short, the mutinies were informed by a consciousness of a project of power, most obviously manifest in the singular way the sepoys wanted to destroy their dominators. All these features have parallels with the general features of peasant insurgency in the colonial period.[41] The sepoys were, in fact, behaving in exactly the same way as the peasants behaved when they took to arms time and again, against the dominant triad of *sarkar, sahukar* and *zamindar.*

This similarity is not surprising. All data that we have of the recruitment of the sepoys of the Bengal Army show that they were mostly drawn from the agricultural families of southern Awadh and eastern U.P.[42] This common background explains the easy communication across sepoy lines in north India and also the similar reaction of the sepoys to rumours. The sepoys were, to use a cliche, 'peasants in uniform' and so when they rebelled they did so in exactly the same manner as their brothers in the villages did. This similarity also explains another thing. It puts into perspective the transformation of the mutinies into popular insurgency. Once the mutinies had struck and British administration had collapsed, in

[38]K. Marx, *A Contribution to the Critique of Hegel's Philosophy of Right, Introduction,* in Marx, *Early Writings,* edited by L. Colletti (Harmondsworth, 1975), p. 244.

[39]Mukherjee, *Awadh in Revolt,* p. 87.

[40]Kaye, *Sepoy War 1857–58,* iii, p. 456.

[41]Guha, *Elementary Aspects.*

[42]Mukherjee, *Awadh in Revolt,* pp. 76–79.

the words of one British officer. 'like a house made of cards;'[43] the rebellion spread rapidly in the countryside and among the common people. The common people were waiting for the mutinies to initiate the uprising. In Meerut, to quote the official narrative again:

> Before a shot was fired, the inhabitants of the Sudder Bazar went out, armed with swords, spears, clubs, any weapon they could lay hands on, collected in crowds in every lane and alley, at every outlet of the bazars; and the residents of the wretched hamlets...were to be seen similarly armed, pouring out to share in what they evidently knew was going to happen.[44]

They used these arms, as we have seen, against government property, against the white man, the zamindar and the moneylender. In Kanpur, Nanak Chand described in his diary the plunder of all the houses of the mahajans and the rich.[45] What began as a mutiny transformed itself into a peasant rebellion. The sepoy-peasant continuum explains why the features of the mutiny were so similar to the features of peasant rebellion and also why the sepoys' actions found such a direct and immediate echo in the countryside.

The sepoy, when he revolted, shed his uniform. In Meerut, most of the mutineers were in undress and 'they went to Delhi not, in military array, but in straggling disorder.'[46] In Kanpur, the sepoys broke out of their lines and tore off their regimental colours.[47] In short, the sepoys were rejecting the regimentation that had been imposed on them. The one thing they refused to surrender from their days in the Bengal Army was, of course, their arms. The peasant in uniform became the peasant with arms.

The rejection of the uniform and regimentation also has, perhaps, a greater significance. The act of mutiny was an act of negation, an act to eliminate individuals and a form of government that was seen as a threat to the social order. But this negation even if it replicated the violence of the masters was not a mere inversion, an empty act of imitation. In the rejection of the

[43]Gubbins, *Mutinies* p. 118.

[44]*Narrative of Events*, Meerut, p. 251, para 155.

[45]Nanak Chand's diary of events in Kanpur: printed as 'Translation of a Narrative of Events of Cawnpore', in *Narrative of Events in the NWP in 1857–58* (Calcutta, n.d.).

[46]*Narrative of Events*, Meerut, p. 253, para 184.

[47]'Synopsis of the Evidence of the Cawnpore Mutiny', in *Narrative of Events*, Kanpur; see also G.W. Forrest, *Selections from Letters*, ii, Intro, pp. 156–58.

uniform, the regimentation, the colours—all those various signs by which an alien order had tried to separate the sepoy from his peasant brethren—there is the quest, however faint or groping, of an alternative identity which was perhaps entrenched in the shared common world of the peasantry. The alternative lay in that commonality and it was that sense of collectivity that provided the uprising with its ultimate source of strength.

The Residency after Shelling
Courtesy: *Malavika Karlekar (Private collection)*

It is said that the Union Jack did not go down in the Residency in Lucknow till the midnight of 14–15 August 1947. Throughout the rebellion of 1857, when in most parts of the Gangetic plain British rule had ceased to exist, the British held out in the Residency. They were surrounded on all sides by rebel forces who shelled the building and ruined it. The British endured terrible hardship—loss of lives and lack of food and drinking water. The defence of the Residency became a synonym for British heroism. The Residency was relieved and the remnants of the garrison rescued first by Outram and Havelock and then again by Colin Campbell. The picture shows the state of the Residency after it had been shelled by the rebels.

Two Intellectual Traditions of the Revolt of 1857: A Study of Popular Resistance

My book *Awadh in Revolt* was born under a cusp. It was published in 1984 but the text was completed in early 1983. It thus missed the full impact of the most important intervention in modern Indian historiography, the shift in thinking initiated by *Subaltern Studies* and Ranajit Guha's *Elementary Aspects of Peasant Insurgency in Colonial India* (1983). My text could do no more than include a passing reference to the first volume of *Subaltern Studies*, published in 1982. There were themes in my book which could have been enriched from the perspective opened up by Guha and his colleagues, and most of the recent writings on 1857—as neglected a field now as it was in the late 1970s and early 1980s—have followed lines suggested in the writings of Guha and others in the Subaltern Studies collective. This essay will look at some of these developments.

There were two formative intellectual influences on my text. One was immediate and obvious. This came directly from the writings of Eric Stokes on the revolt of 1857. These marked, as the preface to the first edition indicated, the starting points of my enquiry, and some of Stokes's conclusions were also the targets of my critique. The other influence was the history-from-below approach of E.P. Thompson, Christopher Hill, George Rude and Rodney Hilton. I drew inspiration from the writings of these historians and tried to use some of their methods. This seemed valid at the time. But as I read more of the writings of some of the scholars of the Subaltern Studies collective and reflected on the implications of their work,

This essay appeared as the Introduction in *Awadh in Revolt 1857–1858: A Study of Popular Resistance* (Delhi, 2001).

I recognised that they were pushing me to think beyond history-from-below and some of the other accepted shibboleths of radical historiography.

Soon after the appearance of *Awadh in Revolt* came the publication of Eric Stokes's posthumous book *The Peasant Armed.*[1] This was not a finished work and it did not have the section that Stokes wanted to write on Awadh. The general thrust of Stokes's analysis as revealed in his earlier articles[2] was strengthened by the pieces Bayly had put together in *The Peasant Armed.* Stokes urged that it was more important to look at local differentiae in the revolt than seek linkages and connections. Until the local differences were set out district by district, historians would be 'striking matches in the dark'.[3] This was based on an overall scepticism about the possibilities of generalisations in history. 'Historical truth,' Stokes averred, 'marches only briefly to tunes of sounding generality.'[4] My book tried to show the inadequacies of such a disaggregated view of the rebellion. There is no need here to rehearse those arguments. But it is important to recall the fact that Stokes's book gave a pivotal role to the peasantry.

All the great issues of interpretation of 1857, Stokes said, turned on the assessment of peasant action. The peasantry formed the vital link between military mutiny and rural turbulence. 'In a real sense,' he wrote, 'the revolt was essentially the revolt of a peasant army breaking loose from its foreign masters.'[5] But this assignation of a central role to peasants was not matched by any gesture towards making peasants masters of their own destiny. Peasants were invariably the objects of one thing or the other—land-revenue policy or some other policy on the part of the colonial state or the local landlord or usurer. The actions of peasants in the great rebellion were not informed by any consciousness: their actions were determined by local magnates, dominant peasants, or worse by designing men, all of whom turned instinctively against

[1]Eric Stokes, *The Peasant Armed: The Indian Revolt of 1857*, edited by C.A. Bayly (Oxford, 1986).

[2]These articles are available in Eric Stokes, *The Peasant and the Raj: Studies in Agrarian Society and Peasant Rebellion in Colonial India* (Cambridge, 1978).

[3]*Peasant Armed*, p. 225. On page 14 he wrote, 'The nature of the rural uprising in Upper India needs to be looked at more narrowly and its local differentiae observed.'

[4]Ibid., p. 14.

[5]Ibid.

their 'natural enemies' once the structure of the colonial state had collapsed under the onslaughts of the native soldiery.[6]

It was precisely here that Guha's *Elementary Aspects*[7] taught us to look and to think anew about peasants in revolt. Guha located the peasantry in colonial India within a relationship of power, in a relationship of domination and subordination. On one side were the dominators—the triumvirate of *sarkar*, *sahukar* and zamindar—and on the other the subordinated peasantry. Implicit in this pairing or opposition of power was the autonomous subjectivity of the dominated, the peasants. For if the peasants were not autonomous and un-dominated, the dominators, in the very exercise of their domination, would suppress and obliterate the dominated. Domination would thus be left without its Other. The peasantry thus had to be given its own autonomous domain. Guha argued that this domain could be located in what was opposed to domination, i.e. resistance. It was in resistance that the peasantry became conscious of the dominator and of its own autonomous identity.[8]

Then peasants revolted, the dominators were forced to recognise them. Insurgent peasants forced their way into the historical archives created and preserved by dominators. By reading this archive against its grain, the historian would gain access not only to the actions of peasants but also to the consciousness that informed those actions. Peasants had too much at stake to take to arms in a fit of absent mindedness. The archive of the dominator preserved, in a mirror image, the consciousness of the dominated who were powerless to record their own actions, perceptions and knowledge.[9] Guha's aim was not to depict the struggle of peasants as a series of specific encounters but in its general form. He sought to isolate the ideological invariants of peasant consciousness: he called them 'elementary aspects'. There were six such: negation, ambiguity, modality, solidarity, transmission and territoriality. To illustrate these aspects, Guha drew on an enormous amount of historical material, which inevitably meant from the events of 1857, in which the peasants had played such a crucial and important part.

[6]Ibid., pp. 214–25.

[7]Ranajit Guha, *Elementary Aspects of Peasant Insurgency in Colonial India* (Delhi, 1983).

[8]Ibid., Introduction.

[9]Ibid.; also see R. Guha, 'The Prose of Counter-insurgency', in R. Guha (ed.), *Subaltern Studies II* (Delhi, 1983).

Peasants, Guha wrote, could recognise themselves and form their own identity through an act of negation of their superiors. This negative consciousness was expressed first through discrimination—peasants selected the targets of their violence—and then extension—peasants extended their violence to all that was associated with their enemies. In 1857, *banias* and *mahajans* were the victims of attacks and were ousted from land. Guha cited examples from Muzaffarnagar and Hamirpur. In 1857 peasants destroyed and plundered the properties of Europeans and did relatively less damage to those of natives. The violence was extended by the logic of association, in the words of one British official, to everything 'with which we are connected', prisons, record rooms, factories, the telegraph, railways stations, the courts and so on were all targets of attack.[10] The other form of the expression of negation was inversion. Peasants asserted their resistance by appropriating for themselves the signs of authority that belonged to the dominator. They sought to invert the terms of domination and subordination. Rebellion violated the established codes of deference. In 1857 the sepoys, in station after station, became more and more insolent towards their superior white officers before they finally took to arms. British women taken as prisoners after the massacre at Satichaura Ghat in Kanpur were made to grind corn. Mahomed Ali Khan, an influential person in Kanpur known as the Nuneh Nawab and as a friend of the British, had his horse taken away and was given a mule belonging to a servant. Dominators became the objects of humiliation and abuse which were normally directed towards the dominated.[11]

This inversion of the codes of dominance and subordination during insurgency often meant that rulers were liable to misread the signs of rebellion as crime. This gave to insurgency a degree of ambiguity, the second of the aspects Guha analysed. But crime and insurgency 'derive from two different codes of violence': 'unlike crime, peasant rebellions are necessarily and invariably public and communal events ... the criminal may be said to stand in the same relation to the insurgent as does what is conspiratorial (or secretive) to what is public (or open) or what is individualistic (or small-group)

[10]See Guha, *Elementary Aspects*, pp. 20–25.

[11]For inversion see ibid., pp. 28ff; sepoy insolence is well documented, Guha gives instances on p. 39. The Kanpur examples are from Rudrangshu Mukherjee, *Spectre of Violence: The 1857 Kanpur Massacres* (Delhi, 1998), chapter entitled 'The Event'.

to what is communal (or mass) in character.'[12] Unable to recognise the distinction between crime and rebellion and the moment when the former becomes the latter, officials in 1857 labelled all rebels as dacoits—as if the two words were synonymous. Guha gave examples of this confusion and ambiguity.[13] There was a warning in Guha's text to stop the historian from thinking like a *daroga*.

Destruction was the principal modality or form of peasant insurgency. Guha identified four forms of destruction: wrecking, burning, eating and looting; the violence was also public, collective and total.[14] The public and collective character of the revolt of 1857 is obvious from the reports available of *panchayats* and discussions that preceded the call to arms.[15] In Kanpur, the rebels met before the uprising to discuss things, and General Wheeler in the entrenchment was actually informed that the attack on the entrenchment was about to begin. Even the decision to massacre the British on the river was taken collectively.[16] Wrecking, burning and looting were extensive in 1857. The British and those seen as their friends had their property and their insignias of authority destroyed and plundered. A representative description was cited by Guha from Mark Thornhill's account of the sack of Mathura: 'The plunder of the revenue office was followed by that of the English houses. In this amusement the villagers spent what remained of the day. The houses contained little that they valued; that little they carried off, the rest they broke to pieces. In the morning they returned and continued the work of destruction.'[17] Fire was the principal instrument of destruction. Recalling a series of fires that destroyed a cantonment, a bungalow and a telegraph office, at Ranigunj and Barrackpore, W.H. Carey wrote in retrospect, 'the Fire King began to demonstrate an inkling of what was in store for almost every station in the North Western Provinces.' In the summer of 1857, across the plains of north India, it was arson that destroyed record rooms, session courts, bungalows, post offices, and so on.[18] The public character of the insurgency was also expressed in the setting up of a rebel authority with power to

[12] *Elementary Aspects*, p. 79.
[13] Ibid., pp. 101ff.
[14] Ibid., ch. 4.
[15] Ibid., pp. 118–19.
[16] Mukherjee, *Spectre of Violence*, pp. 49–51 and 70–1.
[17] *Elementary Aspects*, pp. 138–9.
[18] Ibid., pp. 140–1.

impose laws, sanctions and punishments. In 1857, as is well known, this meant harking back to the pre-British order.

Solidarity, Guha wrote, was the categorical imprint of rebel consciousness. Its quality could vary but no rebellion was without it. Solidarity to the rebel cause in 1857 showed itself in the steadfast refusal of common people to collaborate with British authorities. When the magistrate of Saharanpur entered the village of Manuckpur to arrest its headman, he found the village 'all but deserted' despite a large read for the apprehension of the headman.[19] In Awadh, as I had shown, villagers withheld supplies to the advancing British army.[20] Even after their victory the British, in the course of their enquiry into the events, found it difficult to establish facts and find names of rebels because the people refused to come forward with evidence.[21]

One indicator of the strength of this solidarity was the speed with which the message of rebellion was transmitted, leaving the rulers bewildered. This touches upon the two best-known features of the revolt of 1857: the circulation of the *chapati*, and rumours. Nobody has been able to explain the significance of the circulating chapati. There is no trace left in the records of the meaning attached to it by the peasants of 1857. The British did not know what to make of it, but after the event some bureaucrats and scholars used it as a convenient peg on which to hang their conspiracy theory. T. Rice Holmes, in fact, compared the chapatis to the 'fiery cross that summoned the clans-men of Roderick to battle.' They misread, as Guha points out, a symbol as an index and the chapati became the transmitter of the message of conspiracy and revolt. But there were local administrators in 1857 who were not willing to endow the chapati any such significance. For them, in the words of Guha, 'the chapati was more of a red herring than a fiery cross.' Guha, however, brought to the chapati phenomenon a new angle. He showed, via William Crooke's observations of rural life in northern India, that during an epidemic some ritually consecrated object was circulated to push the disease outside the boundaries of a village or a locality. This technique was called *chalawa* which means, according to Crooke, passing on the malady'. North India had witnessed a

[19]Ibid., pp. 206–7.

[20]Mukherjee, *Awadh in Revolt*, ch. 4.

[21]Guha, *Elementary Aspects*, pp. 213–14; and Mukherjee, *Spectre of Violence*, p. 109.

cholera epidemic and the chapati could have been the traditional chalawa. But the chapati could have meant different things to different people. Guha summed up thus:

> The symbolic agent of an epidemic in the countryside it [the chapati] took on an added meaning as the carrier of an imminent but undefined political holocaust ... As an omen it looked ahead of events, and in an atmosphere charged with growing unrest in agrarian communities and army barracks it transmitted the rebellion in anticipation by sounding a tocsin for all to hear but none to understand why.[22]

Guha analysed rumours as both a 'universal and necessary carrier of insurgency in any pre-industrial, pre-literate society'. The power of rumours is acknowledged in the efforts the authorities put in to suppress and control their circulation. But rumours had more to them than the alarm engendered among those who had most to lose from a popular uprising. It helped spread the message of rebellion: it was a trigger and a mobiliser, a necessary instrument of rebel transmission. Rumours, by definition, are anonymous and verbal. The latter feature gives to rumours functional immediacy which allows it to seize upon important issues in periods of social tension. Rumours have a socialising process embedded in them since the passing on of a rumour, in the words of one authority, 'involves a desire on the part of the transmitter to affect other people's behaviour, to bring their perspectives in line with his own, or, at the very minimum, to share a valuable piece of information.' It is to this 'comradeship response' that rumours owe their remarkable speed. Characteristically, rumours originate and circulate where people assemble in large numbers. Kaye, in the context of 1857, described rumours as 'the lies of the Bazaar'. As any student of the great rebellion knows, Kaye drew on material linking the rumours in circulation in the bazaars with the spreading disaffection among the sepoys. Rumours can never be pinned down, they are by nature ambiguous. Kaye mentioned the vernacular saying 'It is in the air'. This, according to Guha, is what makes rumours 'a mobile and explosive agent of insurgency'. Rumours are open because they are anonymous and unverifiable; they are transitive and free; their

[22]For Guha's discussion on the chapati, see ibid., pp. 238–46; all quotations in this paragraph are from these pages.

circulation is unpremediated and therefore liable to improvisation. In 1857, rumours about greased cartridges soon spread to include edible items like flour and ghee, and then to a general conspiracy to defile and convert the entire population of India. Thus rumours brought sepoys and civilians together by a common suspicion.[23]

Together with chapatis and rumours, prophecies circulated in 1857. The most important of the prophecies was the one that said British power would be destroyed on the centenary of the battle of Plassey. Rumours were the carriers of such prophecies. It made rebels the agents of forces outside and independent of themselves. Rebels saw their destiny as a function of others' wills and actions. Drawing on Marx, Guha described such attitudes as a 'product of self-alienation', a characteristic false consciousness of the period which made the rebel look upon his own act of resistance as a manifestation of another's will.[24]

Peasant rebellions were invariably confined to a particular locality. This led Guha to look at territoriality as the final aspect of peasant insurgency. Territoriality was not always a limiting factor in rebel mobilisation. Guha illustrated this by drawing on the events of the great rebellion of 1857. The mutiny of the sepoys spread swiftly beyond the cantonments and acquired local bases. These bases became the targets of British counterinsurgency campaigns. The locality of the rebellion was defined by the domain of the local enemies—the sarkar and the sahukar. Official buildings, and all that was seen to be associated with British power in an area, became targets, as did the property of the moneylender. Thus the limits of the rebellion's geographical space were determined by a principle of exclusion, by the rebels' perception of the spread of their enemies' authority and power. It was also informed by a notion of ethnic space. In north India, where the revolt was concentrated, large populations belonging to the same caste lived in contiguous areas and had perpetuated this territorial arrangement through ritual and kinship. In 1857, ethnic groups articulated their solidarity through rebellion. Various Rajput clans rose en masse. Guha illustrated this with the example of the Bundelas, the Mewatis, the Gujars, and so on. From Awadh, one could add the names of the Bais, the Bachgotis, and others. Most of the villages were single-caste settlements and

[23]Guha discusses rumours in ibid., pp. 251–68; all quotations in this paragraph are from these pages.

[24]Ibid., pp. 268–77.

'these village-based primordial ties were the principal means of rebel mobilisation ... A local insurrection, whatever its immediate cause, tended invariably to adapt itself to the existing pattern of ethnic solidarity in a given area.' But Guha was also quick to note that the territoriality of a revolt was not always marked by a coincidence of its domain and a caste region. A locality larger than a village—a *pargana*, or a district—could be the site of the uprising, with more than one caste taking to arms. Guha made a detailed analysis of the revolt of Meghar Singh in Ghazipur to make this point. Drawing from Awadh one could say that an entire principality could be the site of the revolt and powerful Rajput *talukdars* could leave their villages and their *ilaqa* and go with their men to fight under the banner of Birjis Qadr in Lucknow.[25]

Guha's analysis of some aspects of the revolt of 1857 firmly situated the rebellion as a project of power. It served also to free the subject from the coils of causality. All previous work on the subject, including Stokes's and my own on Awadh, had tried to understand the uprising in terms of its background or its context. Guha tried to emphasise *how* the rebels had acted was as significant, if not more significant, than *why* they had acted. They were not always objects of this or that policy. It was invariably assumed that the act of rebellion would become comprehensible if the material context was fully laid out. Guha, on the other hand, looked at the actions of the rebels rather than at the context of their actions. He saw them as conscious agents working to overturn a power structure that they considered alien, exploitative and oppressive. This insight brought a new dimension to the study of the great uprising.

For the historian of 1857, Guha's emphasis on peasants as conscious agents in the making of their own history focussed attention on the fact that the sepoys who had mutinied were of peasant stock. The peasant origins of the sepoy army had been noted but not elaborated in chapter 3 of *Awadh in Revolt*. I had drawn attention to the importance of Awadh, especially Baiswara, as a recruitment ground for sepoys. Subsequent research on the sepoy army by Seema Alavi tends to confirm these suggestions.[26] The

[25]Guha's analysis of territoriality and the revolt of 1857 will be found in ibid., pp. 308,-32; this paragraph is a bald summary of his rich analysis; the quoted lines will be found on pp. 316–17.

[26]Alavi, *The Sepoys and the Company: Tradition and Transition in Northern India 1770–1830* (Delhi, 1995).

peasant origins of the sepoys facilitated the swift merging of sepoys with peasants after the mutinies. But the specific contribution of the sepoy element to the uprising needs to be reiterated. The sepoys were in a unique position. Apart from the princes and talukdars, they were the only people to have been been proximate to state power. As sons of the peasantry, they had left the village for the world; now, during the revolt, they were bringing the world back to the village. As peasants, they had seen peasants as mere objects of officialdom: as sepoys they could identify the state as the real object of hatred. The sepoys' proximity to state power had a dual aspect. On the one hand, they could identify the state as the enemy. On the other, the same exposure and experience, especially the many battles they had fought in India on behalf of the British, had forced on them the realisation that, in the conduct of war, leadership, discipline and structures of command were crucial. The return of the sepoys to their villages as an armed peasantry was thus informed by a new consciousness. The invoking of the traditional leadership could be a product of that consciousness. It is significant that in 1857 dethroned kings or dispossessed princes—Bahadur Shah, Nana Sahib, Rani Lakshmibai, Birjis Qadr and so on—that is, those who previously established claims to leadership and command, were chosen to give the uprising legitimacy. An older and legitimate political order had lost out to the British or had had their power usurped by the British in the late eighteenth and early nineteenth centuries; the sepoys, in their quest for legitimacy, leadership and command, were reviving that order and fighting a war on its behalf and in its name.[27] Further, as Alavi points out, the re-emergence of these centres of power meant that for the sepoys 'the Company ceased to be the most attractive employer in India and patrons amongst the rebel leaders were able to hold to them [the sepoys] the material, political and ritual inducements which the Company had once monopolised.'[28] Thus the former princes who emerged as leaders, often under popular pressure, were dependent on the sepoys for their fighting power and survival. But the sepoys too were tied to the princes for their livelihood and survival. Such ties gave the rebellion its strength and solidarity.

Stokes suggested—in a remarkable reconstruction of the military dimension of the revolt from the sepoy army's perspective—that

[27]This paragraph is based on what I wrote in *Spectre of Violence*, pp. 65–66.
[28]Alavi, *Sepoys and the Company*, p. 296.

by moving towards Delhi, Lucknow and Kanpur—in other words to fight under the regional leaders—in the initial and crucial phase of the revolt, the sepoys gave up what could have been their tactical strength, a war of movement.[29] The successful attacks on these centres by the British, especially Delhi, led to a collapse in organisation. The sepoy regiments had lost their white officers and had not replaced them with native ones. This, not lack of courage, explains the overall lack of success.[30] The harking back to the kings and princes was thus not without a drawback. But as Tapti Roy, in her study of the revolt in Bundelkhand, has noted pertinently, soldiers in mutiny, whatever their origins, do not stop being soldiers after they have mutinied. An army by definition is an arm of the state and a rebel army stakes its legitimacy by declaring its loyalty to a political authority.[31] Rebel sepoys in 1857 did so by announcing that they were fighting for the Mughal emperor or for Birjis Qadr or Nana Sahib and so on. This declaration of allegiance and loyalty often closed options for the princes and many of them were forced to accept the mantle of leadership under tremendous popular pressure.[32]

This harking back to an older political order reintroduced the question of the ideology of the revolt, which had been a subject of discussion in *Awadh in Revolt*. Some historians have seen patriotism as the driving force behind the rebellion. They have argued that the rebels were motivated by something more than a desire to bring back the eighteenth-century Mughal order and princely power. There was a discernible attachment to a wider entity that went beyond the confines of class, caste, community and village. That overarching entity could be *din* or *dharma*.[33] Rajat Ray has given this argument

[29]Stokes, *Peasant Armed*, ch. 2.

[30]Ibid., p. 98.

[31]Tapti Roy, *The Politics of a Popular Uprising: Bundelkhand in 1857* (Delhi, 1994), pp. 44–45.

[32]For an analysis of how this worked in the case of Nana Sahib, see Mukherjee, *Spectre of Violence*, pp. 63–64; and for the Rani of Jhansi, see Roy, *Bundelkhand*, pp. 103–4.

[33]See Rajat Ray, 'Race, Religion and the Realm: The Political Theory of the "Reigning Indian Crusade", 1857', in N. Gupta and M. Hasan (eds), *India's Colonial Encounter: Essays in Memory of Eric Stokes* (Delhi, 1993), pp. 133–82; and C.A. Bayly, 'Patriotism and Ethical Government, *c.* 1780–1860' in *Origins of Nationality in South Asia: Patriotism and Ethical Government in the Making of Modern India* (Delhi, 1998), pp. 86ff

a sharper edge by suggesting that the consistent invocation to Hindus and Mussalmans in all the proclamations that came out of the rebel camps was a precursor to 'the Indian nation' which the Congress leaders invoked in the 1920s.[34] The only difficulty in this interpretation is that the actions and motives of rebels come to be seen through the filter of terms and concepts which were perhaps unknown to them.

To the 'non-question'[35] of whether the revolt was retrograde or forward looking, Chris Bayly in his book on empire and information has introduced a new dimension.[36] He has shown that just as the British used a variety of communication channels and information-gathering networks to facilitate their counter-insurgency operations, the rebels too showed a remarkable degree of awareness about the importance of communication in the success of a rebellion. As is well known, one of the first things they did was cut the telegraph wires. In some places they even cut off postal communications along the Grand Trunk Road. The road, in fact, became the site for a battle to keep the *dak* running. Rebel leaders also used the customary mode of placards near mosques. There were also proclamations; and rebels even used forms of modern media. There were anti-British newspapers and 'the whole panoply of written indigenous communication—*akhbarats*, *charitas*, *parwanas*, *roznamachas* and the like—were employed to spread the message of revolt and the restoration of the authority of the King of Awadh.' The rebel court in Lucknow kept meticulous records and had its own team of writers and *munshis*. The rebel leadership in Awadh used the printing press: 'the most important proclamation of early August 1857 was lithographed.' Rebels also had their own counter-intelligence system and they restored the *harkara* system.[37] Rebels by no means abhorred modern methods of communication.

The year of the rebellion also saw a sudden blooming of Indian medicine and astrology, forms of knowledge that the British had sought to marginalise on account of their interest in spreading English education and Western science. One Pandit Hari Chander reportedly incited rebels with his 'knowledge of the stars and the

[34]Ray, 'Race, Religion and Realm', p. 166.

[35]The very apt epithet is Tapti Roy's: *Bundelkhand*, p. 258.

[36]C.A. Bayly, *Information and Empire: Intelligence-Gathering and Social Communication in India, 1780–1870* (Cambridge, 1996).

[37]The facts and the quotations are taken from ibid., pp. 320–24.

occult sciences'. Native doctors came in to dress the wounds of soldiers. The revolt thus became a battleground of ideas.[38] But the ideas of those who lost are not adequately documented in the available archives.[39] There was in 1857, one could say invoking Foucault, 'an insurrection of subjugated knowledges'.[40] These were popular knowledges disqualified from the hierarchy of knowledges and sciences. Their reappearance and articulation constituted a critique of British rule and of the intellectual apparatus it imposed on Indians to justify and perpetuate its domination.[41] This battle of ideas was inevitably one-sided because a fully embodied intellectual system was attacked by 'a local.. [and] a differential knowledge incapable of unanimity,[42] But an awareness of this conflict is important because it disrupts a process of appropriation by which the uprising of 1857 is made a part of the grand narrative of Indian nationalism and the making of a modern Indian state.

[38]Ibid., pp. 329–30.

[39]There is the possibility that this perspective might be factually enhanced from Urdu and Persian sources. A step has been taken in this direction by the History Department of Aligarh Muslim University. Some of their initial findings were put together in an issue of *Social Scientist*, vol. 26, nos 1–4 (Jan-April, 1998), devoted to the revolt of 1857.

[40]M. Foucault, 'Two Lectures' in *Power/Knowledge: Selected Interviews and Other Writings, 1972–1977*, edited by Colin Gordon (New York, 1980), p. 81. Bayly (p. 330) uses the phrase but does not work out the implications.

[41]Ibid., p. 82.

[42]Ibid.

Postcard company: Attar Chand and Co. Dariba Kalan, Delhi. Likely 1930s based on quality, could also be 1920s.

Mutiny Memorial (Delhi)
Courtesy: *Aditi Chandra (Private collection)*

The battle for Delhi was one of the key episodes in the annals of the rebellion. Delhi fell to the rebels between 11 and 13 May. The British did not completely recover the city till the beginning of October 1857. In between this period the old Mughal capital was the site of bloodshed and plunder. The taking of Delhi was seen by the British as a major triumph. Once the rebellion had been suppressed all over North India the British began the process of memorializing the event. One of the ways they did this was through erecting monuments: one such was the Mutiny Memorial Monument pictured above which was set up in 1863. Once begun the process continued and the government of India after independence renamed the monument as a memorial to the vanquished.

Responses to 1857 in the Centenary Year

The centenary of the revolt of 1857 saw the publication of two outstanding books on the uprising. One, by S.N. Sen, was officially sponsored by the government of India and the other by S.B. Chaudhuri was independently researched and published. This essay seeks to contrast the approach and the emphasis of the two books, both of which were written under the influence of nationalism. The authors used and read the existing archives very differently and tried to come to terms with the idea that the uprising was a war of independence.

Anniversaries seldom go unnoticed in India. The centenary of 1857 and its 150th year are certainly no exceptions to this generalisation. But there is a difference in the manner in which the government of India decided to remember the centenary and the manner in which it is celebrating the 150th anniversary. There was a march of young men and women from Meerut that reached Delhi on 11 May 2007. The prime minister and other luminaries spoke to the nation on 11 May from the Red Fort. The date for the beginning of the uprising was quietly shifted from 10 May to 11 May, presumably because it was only on the latter date that the sepoys from Meerut reached Delhi and the rebellion commenced there. How could a war of independence have begun in Meerut? It makes it look so much better to make it begin, with a small sleight of hand, in Delhi! Even earlier, a finance minister not known for his generosity had promised considerable amounts of largesse for organising seminars, exhibitions and so on.

The mood in 1957 was remarkably different. There was a celebration, of course. However, India's first prime minister,

This essay appeared in the *Economic and Political Weekly*, Vol XLIII, no. 24, June 14, 2008.

Jawaharlal Nehru, unwilling perhaps to even unwittingly don the mantle of the last Mughal emperor, Bahadur Shah Zafar, did not speak from the Red Fort but addressed a meeting at the Ram Lila grounds on 10 May. Two years before that, the minister for education in 1955, Abul Kalam Azad, had announced at the meeting of the Indian Historical Records Commission that he had requested the renowned historian of the Marathas, Surendra Nath Sen, to write a one-volume history of the revolt of 1857. This was published in 1957and today it is known as S. N. Sen's *1857*, a standard reference book on the subject. The government in 1957, thus, chose to give a scholarly dimension to its own involvement in the centenary of the uprising. Two other Indian historians also published their own interpretations of the great rebellion in 1957. One was Ramesh Chandra Majumdar, who wrote *The Sepoy Mutiny and the Revolt of 1857* and the other was S.B. Chaudhuri, *Civil Rebellion in the Indian Mutinies (1857–59)*. Even after 50 years, it can hardly be denied that these three works were outstanding contributions to the scholarly literature on 1857. Much of what we say and write about 1857 today is possible because of the work of these three scholars and of the great narratives produced in the second half of the 19th century and early 20th century by Charles Ball, John Kaye, G.W. Forrest and others.

TENSION WITHIN THE NATIONALIST ASSESSMENT

In this paper I want to focus on the books by Sen and Chaudhuri and to contrast their approaches. But before I come to the writings of these historians, I want to try to locate a tension within the nationalist assessment of the revolt of 1857. Let me begin by taking Jawaharlal Nehru's *The Discovery of India* as a benchmark. Published in March 1946, it has been described by Nehru's biographer, S. Gopal, as an attempt 'to portray an emotional comprehension of Indian nationalism'; it sought, according to Gopal, to so depict India's past as to draw lessons for its future.[1] *The Discovery of India* had a small section entitled 'The Great Revolt of 1857'. Nehru wrote here, 'It was much more than a military mutiny and it spread rapidly and assumed the character of a popular rebellion and a war of Indian independence.' A sentence after this summing up, Nehru commented, 'essentially it was a feudal outburst'. This last qualification made it possible for Nehru to analyse some of the

[1]S. Gopal, *Jawaharlal Nehru: A Biography* (Cape, London, 1975), p. 299.

drawbacks of the uprising. Nehru spoke of the lack of unity among the feudal chiefs, their lack of any constructive ideal or community of interest. He asserted that the feudal chiefs 'had already played their role in history and there was no place for them in the future'. Many of them, Nehru said, were opportunistic and 'stood apart waiting to see on which side victory lay. Many played the part of Quislings.'[2] It will not be unfair to draw the conclusion from Nehru's comments that in his eyes, the feudal aspect of the uprising, which was essential to it, acted as a restraining element on the popular rebellion and the war of independence aspects of the revolt. Nehru detected but did not quite articulate a tension between the feudal and the popular elements of the uprising. The latter wanted to take the uprising towards a war of independence and the former pulled it back.

A decade later, on the centenary of the revolt, when Nehru spoke at the Ram Lila maidan, this tension between the war of independence and the feudal elements had all but disappeared. A hundred years later, according to the first prime minister of India, 1857 had to be remembered as a War of Independence (and as if to emphasise the point, the editor of the relevant volume of Nehru's *Selected Works* capitalised the W of war and the I of independence).[3] This shift in emphasis—perhaps brought about by the demands of political rhetoric—has a bearing on the understanding of the work of S. N. Sen to which I now turn.

Sen's Objective Approach

Sen was given a clear brief and we know about the brief from the foreword Azad wrote to the volume. Azad felt that the 'time had now come to write a new and objective history of the movement of 1857'. The book would be an 'authoritative account' written from the 'standpoint of a true historian', 'based on facts and facts alone and avoid all appeal to passion or sentiment'. The brief followed from Azad's premise that no 'objective history' of the struggle existed. Sen's book was expected to fill this void. Sen echoed these attitudes in his preface whose key phrases were 'dispassionate study' and 'purely objective and scrupulously impartial'. It is surprising, reading the preface today, how even in 1957 Sen took all the claims

[2]J. Nehru, *The Discovery of India* (Calcutta, 1946), p. 383.

[3]*Selected Works of Jawaharlal Nehru*, Second Series, vol. 39 (New Delhi, 2007), pp. 7–11.

about objectivity and impartial history so seriously. Sushobhan Sarkar, in an early review of the book, commented:[4]

> Historical writing ... involves a process of selection from the mass of available facts on the basis of the author's conception of what is important and relevant and what is not; an arrangement of the selected material in a coherent manner; an attempt to draw possible links between different events; a presentation of reflections and inferences which occur to the mind. All these imply point or points of view, an outlook which is the product of a certain experience and environment. It is idle to pretend that one can shake off such points of view.

Sources

The quest for an objective history naturally led Sen to remain very close to his sources. The sources he used were largely written in English and produced by the British. This archive consists of memoirs of serving British officers or of reports prepared by them as part of the counter-insurgency measures. There are also reports of spies, depositions by various participants and reports of committees of inquiry—all produced by the colonial state to suppress the rebellion and to re-establish its power and dominance. Sen also used the great narrative histories of the 19th century written by Kaye, Ball, Rice Holmes, Forrest and so on quite extensively. What is remarkable—and this will remain a bit of a mystery—is that Sen refused to use the Persian and Urdu sources in the National Archives of India (NAI). I use the verb refused advisedly since it is not possible that he did not know of the existence of these documents; after all, he had been head of the NAI and a check-list of these documents had been in print since 1921. He had the resources to have them read and translated but chose not to. Perhaps—and this is only a suggestion—Sen thought that he could not depend on documents that he himself could not read. I make this suggestion because Sen was not averse to using documents in Indian languages that he could himself read. Thus, apart from Bengali, he did use some Marathi material, which he could read as an accomplished historian of the Marathas. What is also worth noting is that Sen did not consult and use the various regional archives, say in Allahabad and Patna. At around the same time that Sen was gathering material for his book

[4]S.C. Sarkar, 'Views on 1857' in *Bengal Renaissance and Other Essays* (New Delhi, 1970), pp. 123–35.

and writing it, S.A. Rizvi and M.L. Bhargava were putting together *Freedom Struggle in Uttar Pradesh* that came out in the centenary year. There was obviously no coordination between Sen's work based in Delhi, Calcutta and London and that of Rizvi and Bhargava based in Allahabad and Lucknow.

Pattern and Causes

Sen followed in the footsteps of Kaye[5] and treated the uprising in terms of administrative divisions or geographical regions. Kaye's second and third volumes, which deal with the actual events of the uprising, have the following divisions: 'The Rising in the North-West', 'Progress of the Rebellion in Upper India', 'The Punjab and Delhi, Bengal, Bihar and the North-West Provinces', 'Mutiny and Rebellion in the North-West Provinces' and a section called 'Lucknow and Delhi'. Sen described the events under the following chapters: 'Delhi', 'Kanpur', 'Oudh', 'Bihar', 'Jhansi', 'Rajputana' and 'Central India' and 'The Punjab'. While this mode of arranging the material was convenient for constructing a narrative, in terms of analysis it could give rise to certain problems. Following this approach, Sen often failed to pick out the links that existed between the events and activities of the rebels in one area with those in another theatre of the rebellion. This made the uprising appear more fractured than it actually was. He arrived at the conclusion that 'nowhere did the sepoy's conduct conform to a common pattern'.[6] Yet, as I have shown in my study of the revolt in Awadh, if one looks at the sepoy mutinies chronologically rather than geographically, it is possible to establish a pattern of movement of the mutinies in the Gangetic plain.[7] Sen assumed that to demonstrate a pattern in the sepoy mutinies would be to suggest that the sepoys had a 'pre-concerted plan to follow'.[8] Detecting a pattern in the actions of the sepoys when they chose to defy and attack their foreign masters is not necessarily to suggest that there was a plan or a conspiracy. Rather it is to show how a group of men from a similar background and with shared experiences driven by a sense of alarm acted in the same way when they chose to mutiny. A pattern is not always a plot.

[5]J.W. Kaye, *History of the Sepoy War, 1857–1858*, 3 vols (London, 1864–1880).

[6]S.N. Sen, *1857* (New Delhi, 1995 (1957)), p. 405. All page references to the 1995 reprint.

[7]Rudrangshu Mukherjee, *Awadh in Revolt, 1857–58: A Study of Popular Resistance* (Delhi, 2001 (1984)), pp. 64–65. All page references to the 1984 edition.

[8]Sen, *1857*, p. 405.

Sen concluded his chapter on the causes of the revolt with the observation, 'The revolt had been long brewing, the greased cartridge only hastened it'.[9] This is a perfectly non-controversial statement but for the fact that Sen made no analysis of the long gestation and its causes. Indeed, in his review of Sen's book from which I have already quoted, Sushobhan Sarkar made the very valid criticism that Sen had completely ignored S.B. Chaudhuri's study of the anti-British movements in India in the century preceding 1857.[10] Chaudhuri's book' had come out in 1955, and it finds no mention in Sen's exhaustive bibliography. Sen made no attempt to link the revolt of 1857 to colonial exploitation and domination. This may have been related to the fact that he was not without sympathy for Britain's work in India. He believed that 'the English government had imperceptibly effected a social revolution. They had removed some of the disabilities of women, they had tried to establish the equality of men in the eye of law, they had attempted to improve the lot of the peasant and the serf'.[12] This assessment of British rule is a trifle surprising from the pen of a historian brought up in the nationalist ethos since it appears to underplay, if not ignore, the indictment of the economic aspects of British rule carried out by early nationalists like Dadabhai Naoroji and R.C. Dutt. That apart, the premise that British rule was the motor of major social changes in India coloured Sen's assessment of the revolt. The rebels had fought against a regime that was committed to establishing modern ideas and institutions. The rebel leaders thus, according to Sen, 'would have set the clock back ... they wanted a counter-revolution'. Sen elaborated as follows, the rebel leadership 'would have done away with the new reforms, with the new order, and gone back to the good old days when a commoner could not expect equal justice with the noble, when the tenants were at the mercy of the talukdars, and when theft was punished with mutilation'.[13] Even in Awadh, where Sen said the revolt had 'assumed a national dimension though the term must be used in a limited sense', the 'patriots' [Sen's word] 'fought for their king and country but they were not champions of

[9]Sen, *1857*, p. 38.

[10]Sarkar, 'Views on 1857', p. 126.

[11]S.B. Chaudhuri, *Civil Disturbances during British Rule in India* (Calcutta, 1955).

[12]Sen, *1857*, p. 414.

[13]Sen, *1857*, p. 414.

freedom for they had no conception of individual liberty ... they would, if they could, revive the old order and perpetuate everything it stood for.'[14] It is clear therefore, that in Sen's mind freedom meant nothing without a conception of individual liberty. Sen was too good an empirical historian to ignore the fact that 'the rebels wanted to get rid of the alien government' but they also wanted to 'restore the old order of which the king of Delhi was the rightful representative'.[15] This seemed to fit awkwardly with what Sen considered to be freedom.

Attitude towards the Rebellion

It will not be unfair to say that Sen's attitude towards the British rule and to the rebellion was no different from the Bengalis of his class in 1857. Most, if not all of them had also felt that the British rule was the harbinger of modernity in India and it had brought in social changes of enormous significance and that the 'sipahis' and the rebels of North India were protesting against these reforms and were therefore, not worthy of support. The loyalty that the western-educated intelligentsia of Calcutta displayed towards British rule in 1857 was subjected to biting satire in 1862 by Kaliprasanna Sinha in *Hootum Pyanchar Naksha*. Sen's text makes it clear that he was not in sympathy with the rebels, their actions and their aspirations. Yet he could not overlook the fact that the rebels had fought to get rid of foreign domination. He thus actually used the phrase 'war of independence' to describe the events of 1857. 'What began as a fight for religion', he wrote, 'ended as a war of independence.'[16] But he could not reconcile the aims and aspirations of this war of independence to his understanding of freedom by which he only understood the liberties achieved by modern nationalism and bourgeois democracy. I will be bold enough to suggest that Sen was influenced, perhaps imperceptibly, by the shift that was taking place in the nationalist attitude towards 1857, a shift that I have tried to capture through the writings and speeches of Jawaharlal Nehru, who was a sensitive student of history. Thus, Sen's almost intuitive antipathy for the aims of the rebels came to be overlaid by the idea of a war of independence. I would venture to say that he could not quite accept the term and so he qualified it by saying that this was not

[14]Sen, *1857*, p. 414.
[15]Sen, *1857*, p. 413.
[16]Sen, *1857*, p. 413.

real freedom. This landed him in a mess of contradictions regarding independence, freedom, individual liberty and so on, contradictions that he did not even try to clarify and resolve.

I will briefly touch upon two other contradictions in Sen's evaluation and analysis of the rebellion. He made the claim that 'no moral issues were involved in the war of 1857'.[17] Yet a few paragraphs earlier he had written that the uprising 'began as a fight for religion'. How a fight for religion could be devoid of moral issues is not clear. The sepoys and the rebels fought in the name of their *dharma* and *deen*. Both the words resonate with moral overtones. Even the rebels' perceptions of their own defeat and failure were imbricated with moral issues. Charles Ball recounted an incident in which a group of rebel sepoys were asked about their failure and they ascribed it to the lack of gratitude they had shown when they had killed their quondam masters. The sepoys said, 'Sahib, it has all been the work of fate. After what we had done, we never could fight. No matter whether your troops were black or white, native or European, we could not stand against them; our salt choked us.'[18] A loss of loyalty, a moral lapse in a world where loyalty and honour mattered, was seen as being the source of a failure of courage. The sepoys were emphatically making a moral statement and since it is recounted in Ball, it could not have been unknown to Sen. He chose to ignore it, perhaps because the moral world of the 'sipahi' was alien to him or distant from him.

I have said earlier that Sen stayed very close to his sources. I want to demonstrate the consequences of this by looking at his chapter on Awadh. The choice of Awadh is to do with my own familiarity with the revolt there, and also because Sen described the uprising there to have acquired some sort of 'national dimension'. The first thing to notice following the footnotes in Sen's chapter is the fact that the narrative is entirely built upon the memoirs of those Britons who were besieged in the Lucknow Residency or were part of the British armies that re-conquered Lucknow and Awadh. There is only one reference to an archival source and this is to a file in the foreign department, secret consultations series kept in the NIA.[19] Sen noted in his bibliography that he had consulted this series, yet there is nothing of significance in the chapter that is actually culled from

[17]Sen, *1857*, p. 414.

[18]C Ball, *The History of the Indian Mutiny*, vol. 2 (London, n.d.), p. 550. The significance of this statement is discussed in Mukherjee, *Awadh in Revolt*, p. 172.

[19]Sen, *1857*, p. 240 n 133.

the files of this series. The overwhelming dependence on memoirs of Britons had an obvious and inevitable result. Sen's chapter on Awadh is actually an account not of the revolt but a description of those who were besieged in the Residency and of how they were relieved by Havelock, Outram and Campbell. The reader will look in vain to find the activities of the rebels, their strength, their strategy and so forth. This is a mystifying lapse since, as I found when doing my own research on Awadh, on the basis of the foreign department, secret consultations, it is possible to build up a fairly detailed account of the rebels and their activities in Awadh. Sen completely ignored this. Thus, we are landed with this peculiar contradiction where an account that sees the rebellion as a war of independence, albeit with some qualifications, does not tell us about the rebels and the rebellion for the very area where Sen said the revolt had acquired a national dimension. From Sen's chapter on Awadh, it is impossible to arrive at the conclusion that the revolt there had a national dimension or that it was a war of independence. The chapter in the manner of Kaye tells the story of British heroism and endurance.

Chaudhuri's Narrative

This was exactly S.B. Chaudhuri's point of departure. He was not concerned with the British, their sufferings and their military triumphs. He was also not concerned with the sepoy mutinies that triggered off the uprising. Two years before 1957, he had published a pioneering monograph describing the manner in which the British rule had been resisted across India in the 100 years preceding the uprising of 1857. His *Civil Rebellion in the Indian Mutinies, 1857–59* was a natural continuation of the 1955 book[20] He wrote,[21]

> These civil disturbances of the earlier period afford a welcome foothold to the historian in evaluating and estimating the civil rebellion of the mutiny period and in discovering that the latter are connected in a long chain of causes with the former and in some cases are even a continuation of them.

The link was not only one of causality but also one of character. According to Chaudhuri, the civil rebellion of the pre-mutiny and

[20] S.B. Chaudhuri, *Civil Rebellion* in *the Indian Mutinies, 1857–59* (Calcutta, 1957).

[21] Chaudhuri, *Civil Rebellion*, pp. xvi–xvii.

the mutiny periods were linked because these were 'primarily anti-British, anti-colonial movements running through feudal channels'.[22]

Chaudhuri had read Sen's work, even though both books came out in the same year and he made the following extremely critical and valid observation. 'Dr Sen's book', he noted, 'which contains a vivid and vigorous account of military activities is less than just to the part played by the general masses of the Indian people in the great upsurge.'[23] The activities of the rebels were precisely what Chaudhuri wanted to capture and thus, fill a significant gap in Sen's narrative of 1857. He set out the purpose of his book thus:[24]

> The following pages, therefore, aim, so far as it is possible to bring within a convenient compass, at presenting the history of the civil rebellion in the Indian mutinies in a connected and indisputably authentic form, its scope and character, the class of people participating in it, and the effect produced in the direction and dimension of this vast conflagration and in the prolongation of the conflict and its consequences.

Sources

How did Chaudhuri propose to construct the activities of the rebels? He wrote that he depended on government records, the narrative of events recorded by British district officers, parliamentary papers, reports, minutes, dispatches and memoranda preserved in what was then the Commonwealth Relations Office in London. He claimed that these records were so voluminous that it minimised the search for unpublished papers or unknown sources. He asserted further that 'fresh materials from untapped sources may only corroborate the approach to the subject taken'.[25] In other words, Chaudhuri read the archives of the victor to arrive at the activities of the rebels. Long before reading sources against their grain or constructing a narrative of insurgency from the prose of counter-insurgency had been theoretically propounded, Chaudhuri, as a good empirical historian, had practised something similar. Lest you think I am making too tall a claim on behalf of Chaudhuri, let me present to you two statements. Here is one from Chaudhuri:[26]

[22]Chaudhuri, *Civil Rebellion*, p. xvii.
[23]Chaudhuri, *Civil Rebellion*, p. xx.
[24]Chaudhuri, *Civil Rebellion*, p. 22.
[25]Chaudhuri, *Civil Rebellion*, p. v.
[26]Chaudhuri, *Civil Rebellion*, pp. v–vi.

> No comprehensive account is available from the defeated side but this limitation in a way enhances the authenticity of the records of the British officers who were compelled in accordance with official orders, to compile a narrative of the mutinies and to acknowledge the genuineness of the popular reaction to the sepoy war ... the account of the Indian rebellion furnished by the British themselves has at least the saving feature that it automatically rules out the charge of biased sources.

Compare this with the following now famous formulation of Ranajit Guha:[27]

> For counter-insurgency, which derives directly from insurgency ... can hardly afford a discourse that is not fully and compulsively involved with the rebel and his activities. It is of course true that the reports, dispatches, minutes, judgments, laws, letters, etc, in which policemen, soldiers, bureaucrats ... and others hostile to insurgency register their sentiments, amount to a representation of their will. But these documents do not get their content from that will alone, for the latter is predicated on another will—that of the insurgent. It should be possible therefore to read the presence of a rebel consciousness as a necessary and pervasive element within that body of evidence.

Might I be bold enough to suggest that the thrust and purport of both these statements are one and the same? Guha says with a great deal of philosophical sophistication what had already occurred to Chaudhuri. The archive of the victors of 1857 by its very nature was forced to record rebel activities and report their movements. Since this corpus of evidence was produced to aid the raj in quelling the revolt it needed to record the rebellion with a degree of authenticity.

Attitude towards the Rebellion

In my discussion of Sen's book, I tried to show with the example of Awadh how he failed to write a history of the rebellion. For Chaudhuri too I will draw on his section on Awadh to try and understand how far he fulfilled his own project. Like Sen, Chaudhuri followed a geographical division except that he went by administrative divisions created by the British. Thus, he treated the events in Awadh under two headings: The Faizabad division and the Lucknow division. He told the story of both these divisions separately

[27] Ranajit Guha, *Elementary Aspects of Peasant Insurgency in Colonial India* (Delhi, 1983), p. 15.

and chronologically. For both the divisions, he showed which of the taluqdars joined the rebellion and their support base. He tried to offer some estimate of the rebel strength at some specific moments of the uprising. The activities of the British came into his account only when they were necessary to explain rebel movements. He told the story of rebel activities and thus, tried to reconstruct a history of the rebellion.[28] He did all this on the basis of sources and documents that were all available to S.N. Sen. The latter had, however, not adequately mined these sources, maybe because he was not as focused on constructing a narrative of rebel activities as Chaudhuri was. This is the principal difference in the approach of the two historians.

We are thus left with something of an anomaly. Sen was asked by the government of India to produce a history of 1857 that would be objective. The premise was that all or most previous histories of 1857 had been written from the British point of view and were therefore, not objective. The demand of objectivity that had been placed on Sen was nothing more than a call to reclaim 1857 for Indian history and Indian historians. But by depending heavily on British memoirs rather than on the archival sources he could have easily used, Sen produced an account that was no different in the story that it told from those told by 19th century British historians. Chaudhuri had no official or state-sponsored brief, even though the then vice-president of India, Sarvepalli Radhakrishnan, wrote a laudatory foreword to the book. Chaudhuri set out to narrate the activities of the rebels and proceeded to do what Sen had failed to do.

Similarity in Approaches

Having emphasised a major difference between the two historians, let me draw attention to one similarity. This concerns the attitude of the two historians towards the religious aspect of the revolt. Both tended to underplay it. Chaudhuri, despite his detailed chronicling and analysis of popular disaffection and rebellion, did not treat religion as a very important factor as a cause of the uprising and as a vehicle for mobilisation. He has a couple of pages on how Hindus and Muslims fought together and of how the various proclamations appealed to both Hindus and Muslims[29] but otherwise kept religion outside his analysis of popular revolt. Sen, as we have seen, said that the uprising began as a fight for

[28]See Chaudhuri, *Civil Rebellion*, pp. 118–43.
[29]See Chaudhuri, *Civil Rebellion*, pp. 218–82.

religion and ended as a war of independence. In this transition from the beginning to the end, religion slipped out of Sen's analytical framework. He made no analysis of the proclamations and spent no time in trying to understand the role that religion had played in the uprising. Every single 'ishtahar' issued by the rebel leadership was formulated in religious terms: They asked the people, Hindus and Muslims, to rise up and fight the 'firanghi'[30] This absence in both historians, otherwise so different in their approaches to 1857, is perhaps not without significance. Will it be an exaggeration to suggest that writing a decade after independence, when secularism had become enshrined in the nation's spirit, they were influenced by that prevailing intellectual and political ambience? An attempt to claim 1857 to that prevailing spirit of secular-nationalism could not quite situate religion as an important element in the revolt.

CONCLUSION

In conclusion, I want to briefly reiterate the point about claiming 1857 for a national ethos. In his last chapter, Sen wrote that the 'heroes of 1857' had fought for independence but under Mahatma Gandhi's national movement India 'had achieved freedom and liberty'.[31] Chaudhuri saw in 1857 a 'curious' coming together of 'old feudal instincts and anti-alien patriotism'. The latter, he said, 'was not yet of the pure advanced political type, as the leaven of feudal discontent was still strong. Yet the yearning for freedom, which was latent in these instincts stood out as the outward emblem of a national outburst against foreign rule.' 'Who knows', he asked in the penultimate sentence of his book, 'that the inception of the nationalist movement was not contained in the rising of 1857 after the fashion of the oak in the acorn?'.[32] For both historians, the revolt of 1857 was linked to the national movement through however jagged a line and however circuitous a route. Chaudhuri harked back to the Nehru of *The Discovery of India*, and saw a tension between the popular uprising and the feudal elements; Sen was closer to Nehru, the prime minister by emphasising that it was a war of independence. The revolt of 1857 with all its power and passion could not be allowed to stand on its own. It had to be made a part of a bigger national narrative.

[30]See Mukherjee, *Awadh* in *Revolt*, pp. 147–54 for an analysis of the religious content of the proclamations.

[31]Sen, *1857*, p. 419.

[32]Chaudhuri, *Civil Rebellion*, pp. 298–99.

An Act of Defiance

***Courtesy**: http://www.heritage-history.com/www/heritage.php?Dir=wars& FileName=wars_indianmutiny.php*

This is an early 20th century drawing of Mangal Pandey's act of defiance. There is no visual record of either Mangal Pandey or his actions that goes back to 1857. This drawing should be seen with that important caveat in mind.

A solitary sepoy on a hot afternoon in March 1857 in Barrackpore attacked his white officers. At his trial he refused to speak. He was hanged. When entire regiments of sepoys all over North India began killing their white officers, they did not speak of the sepoy in Barrackpore, called Mangal Pandey. He seemed to have passed into oblivion till historians rescued him as the man who had begun the trail of blood.

MANGAL PANDEY

BRAVE MARTYR OR ACCIDENTAL HERO?

CHAPTER ONE

29 March 1857

It could have been any ordinary Sunday in the cantonment of Barrackpore. The month was March, an odd time in terms of the weather in Bengal. It was nearly the end of spring. It was hot but summer was still a few weeks away. In the early morning and after sunset a cool breeze came in from the river. John Kaye, who in the 19th century wrote a history of 1857 that even today commands magisterial authority, described the peaceful conditions of Barrackpore in very evocative terms:

> On the banks of the Hooghly River, sixteen miles from Calcutta by land, is the great military station of Barrackpore. It was the headquarters of the Presidency division of the Army ... There, on the green slopes of the river, stood, in a well-wooded park, the country seat of the Governor-General ... As the sun declined on the opposite bank, burnishing the stream with gold, and throwing into dark relief the heavy masses of the native boats, the park roads were alive with the equipages of the English residents. There, visitors from Calcutta, escaping for a while from the white glare and the dust-laden atmosphere of the metropolis, consorted with the families of the military officers ... It was a pleasant, a gay, a hospitable station; and there was not in all India a Cantonment so largely known and frequented by the English.[1]

The sepoy lines in Barrackpore were quiet during the afternoon of 29 March in 1857. Most of the sepoys were lounging around,

This was first published by Penguin Books (India, 2005).

[1]J.W. Kaye, *History of the Sepoy War 1857–58*, i. 494.

and the white officers were in their bungalows enjoying their siesta before preparing to go out with their families to attend evensong. Nobody anticipated that the serenity was about to be disrupted and history about to be made.

In the late afternoon, a sepoy of the 34th Native Infantry, wearing his regimental jacket but in a dhoti instead of the regulation trousers, appeared before the quarter-guard. It was obvious that he was greatly agitated. He had with him a loaded musket and his talwar. He belonged to the 5th Company and his name was Mangal Pandey. He strode around in the quarter-guard, shouting to his comrades. He asked the bugler to sound the assembly and yelled at his comrades to join him: 'Come out, you *bhainchutes*, the Europeans are here! Why aren't you getting ready? It's for our religion! From biting these cartridges we shall become infidels. Get ready! Turn out, all of you! You have incited me to do this and now you *bhainchutes*, you will not follow me!'[2] This kind of open insolence was not common among sepoys, and a naik quickly carried the report of Mangal Pandey's disorderly conduct to Sergeant Major James Hewson. The naik, in his report to his white superior officer, added that Mangal Pandey was under the influence of bhang.

In a few minutes, Hewson was dressed and was at the parade ground. He summoned the jemadar of the company and demanded to know why the sepoy had not been arrested. The jemadar explained his helplessness, 'What can I do?' he said. 'The naik has gone to the adjutant. The havildar is gone to the field officer. Am I to take him myself?'[3] Hewson ordered him to fall in his guard with loaded weapons. Hewson later recalled that some of the men grumbled and that the jemadar did not insist on the men falling in or loading.[4] As the sergeant-major approached Mangal Pandey, the latter took aim and fired. The ball missed Hewson who took shelter behind the bell-of-arms (a bell-shaped building where weapons were stored). A couple of sepoys tried to persuade Mangal Pandey to surrender his weapons. By this time the adjutant, Lieutenant Baugh had arrived on horseback. The incident was now poised to take an even more dramatic turn.

[2]Testimony of Sheikh Paltu quoted in G.W. Forrest, *Selections from the Letters, Despatches and other State Papers Preserved in the Military Department of the Government of India, 1857–58*, 4 vols, i, 124 (henceforth, *Selections*).

[3]*Selections*, i, 117.

[4]Ibid.

Baugh galloped into the quarter-guard shouting, 'Where is he? Where is he?' He was warned by Hewson, 'To your left! Ride to the right, Sir, for your life. The sepoy will fire at you!' Mangal Pandey did exactly that and hit Baugh's horse, which collapsed. Baugh extricated himself, drew one of his pistols from the saddle holster and ran towards Mangal Pandey who was reloading his musket. Baugh fired from around 20 yards and missed. He then drew his sword and rushed towards the sepoy.[5] According to Baugh's recollection, he had proceeded about halfway when Mangal Pandey drew his talwar. Baugh looked back to see where his horse was as he wanted to get his other pistol but the animal had wandered off. He decided to engage the sepoy and he was joined by Hewson, sword in hand.

Hewson's recollection of the encounter is significant enough to be flagged for later consideration. He remembered:

> Mungul Pandy made a cut with a tulwar at me, but did not strike me. He struck the adjutant [Baugh]. The next cut I received myself ... At the same time I was knocked down from behind by one or two blows from a sepoy's musket. I could not recognize the features of the man who struck me; he was regimentally dressed. On rising I advanced again towards. [Pandey] and caught him by the collar of the coat with the left hand. I struck him several times with my sword and received another cut from his tulwar. I was again knocked down from behind.[6]

Baugh, in his turn, had received a cut on his left hand, which disabled it. He had another deep cut on his neck and a gash on the back of his head from a musket butt. More serious harm to Baugh and Hewson was prevented by Sheikh Paltu, a Muslim sepoy, who held Mangal Pandey by his waist while the British officers escaped from what could have been their deaths. The saviour of Baugh and Hewson released Mangal Pandey only when members of the quarter-guard threatened to shoot him if he did not let go of Mangal Pandey.'[7]

The commanding officer of the 34th Native Infantry. Steven Wheler, now appeared in the parade-ground. He ordered the jemadar to arrest the defiant sepoy. The jemadar replied, 'The men

[5] *Selections*, i, 117–18, 121 and 130.
[6] *Selections*, i, 118–19.
[7] Ibid.

won't go.' Wheler repeated the order twice and the jemadar told his men to advance. They proceeded a few paces, stopped and refused to go any further. Wheler realized the futility of trying to enforce his order. He later told the court of inquiry:

> Someone, a native in undress, mentioned to me that the sepoy in front [was] a Brahmin, and that no one would hurt him. I considered it ... a useless sacrifice of life to order a European officer, with the guard, to seize him, as he would no doubt have picked off the European officers, without receiving any assistance from the guard itself. I then left the guard, and reported the matter to the Brigadier.[8]

By now the news of the commotion in the parade ground had reached Major-General John Hearsey who commanded the Presidency Division. The news was brought to him by a lieutenant whose hands and clothes were partly covered in blood.[9] Hearsey called his two sons, who were officers of native infantry regiments, and the three of them left immediately for the parade ground. As they galloped in, they found the parade ground crowded with 'sepoys in their undress and unarmed'. There were some British officers around, including Brigadier Charles Grant and the station commander, Major Ross, but they seemed unable to deal with the problem. The General asked why the sepoy had not been arrested and he was told that the guard would not take orders. Hearsey rode towards the guard with the words, 'We'll see about that.' Someone warned, 'His musket is loaded,' to which Hearsey's retort was 'Damn his musket!' His elder son called out to him, 'Father, he is taking aim at you.' General Hearsey's reply to his son was, 'If I fall, John. rush upon him and put him to death.' Hearsey then rode up to the quarter-guard. He pointed his pistol at the jemadar and said, 'The first man who refuses to march when I give the word is a dead man. Quick march!' He then went towards Mangal Pandey; the guard followed while his sons covered the jemadar with their pistols. It was now Mangal Pandey's turn to act. This is what he did, in the words of Hearsey:

> It appeared the mutineer had suddenly altered his mind, I suppose seeing there was no chance of escape ... He turned the musket muzzle towards his own breast hurriedly, touching the trigger with

[8] *Selections*. i, 147–48.

[9] C. Hibbert, *The Great Mutiny: India, 1857*, 68.

> his toe. The muzzle must have swerved, for the bullet made a deep graze, ripping up the muscles of the chest, shoulder and neck, and he fell prostrate; we were on him at once. The guard calling out—'He has shot himself.' A Sikh sepoy of the guard took his bloody tulwar from under him, for in falling he partly covered his sword with his body. His regimental jacket and clothes were on fire and smoking. I bid the jemadar and the sepoy to put the fire out, which they did ... Dr Hutchinson being present, it was soon ascertained that the wound, though severe was superficial, and the man was conveyed to the hospital ... [10]

One could say that as Mangal Pandey left the parade ground for the hospital, he moved away from history into myth. He did not die of his wounds. He was tried. The verdict was a foregone conclusion. He was hanged a few days later, on 8 April. His actions created a name for the mutinous sepoys of 1857: the British officers called them Pandies.

One incident on a fateful Sunday in March. Was it linked to what was to happen in north India in the summer of the same year? Who was Mangal Pandey and why did he act the way he did? What were the cartridges that he had spoken about? Why did he say he was acting for 'our religion'? These are some of the questions that the rest of the chapters look at.

[10] *Selections*, i, 109–12.

CHAPTER TWO

Life of a Sepoy

Even one hundred and forty-eight years after the event and after a considerable amount of research on the subject, we have little or no precise knowledge about Mangal Pandey. There is a name and there is an action. There is no record about where he came from. Who were his parents? Was he married? When was he recruited and by whom? Answers to all these questions are unknown and speculative. Mangal Pandey has no curriculum vitae to put up to the board of history. He could have preserved this anonymity, like innumerable other sepoys, had he not shot at his superior officers in Barrackpore. His was an unexpected intrusion into history.

The best that can be done to retrieve Mangal Pandey from obscurity is to place him in a particular context. When the English East India Company began to make a bid for political power in south India and in Bengal in the middle of the 18th century, they began recruiting Indian soldiers to strengthen their own meagre armed forces. The number of recruits began to increase as the British embarked on a career of conquest and empire-building in India in the 19th century. The Bengal Army to which Mangal Pandey belonged can be dated roughly to the post-Plassey period when the British began recruiting in Bengal and Bihar to build up a proper army. After his arrival in Calcutta from Madras in late 1756, Robert Clive raised the first battalion of sepoys in Bengal. This consisted of 400 to 500 carefully selected sepoys who were attired in the manner of a British soldier and placed under a British officer to instruct and command them. They came to be known as the Lal Paltan because of the colour of their coat, and later came to be called Galliez (or Gillis) ki Paltan after Captain Primrose Galliez who commanded it for many years. This battalion became the Ist Bengal Native Infantry. After Plassey, Burhanpur and Dinapur became the recruiting grounds for the Company's sepoy army and the recruits were all drawn from rural areas. Very soon the catchment area for recruitment was expanded to include what was then called Awadh and is today eastern Uttar Pradesh and the area around Lucknow. The districts of Rae Bareli, Salon Partapgarh, Sultanpur, Unnao, Faizabad. Gorakhpur and Bahraich supplied a large number of sepoys to the Company's Bengal Army. Recruits from these areas came mostly from the upper castes, especially the Brahmin caste. Mangal Pandey was a typical example.[1]

For the pre-1857 period, however, it is very difficult to find any quantitative estimates of the number of sepoys that came from this area. Awadh was called the 'great nursery for the armies of British India'.[2] In his testimony before the Commission for the Reorganization of the Indian Army, 1859, Colonel Keith Young remarked that 'Oude and the adjacent districts that were formerly under the Oude government furnish about three-fourths of the recruits for the Bengal infantry.'[3] W.H. Sleeman, who toured Awadh extensively in the late 1840s, recorded that southern Awadh (the region called Baiswara) alone provided about 30,000 men to the army in 1825.[4] William Howard Russell of the *Times*, who came to India to report on the revolt, noted in his diary that 'the Byswara district ... furnished in the old days about 40,000 of our finest sepoys to the Bengal army'.[5]

Detailed recruitment data are not available—maybe such data were not recorded. Some stray documents provide a glimpse into the pattern of recruitment. There is a descriptive roll from 1824 of

[1]The early history of the East India Company's army is very well covered in Saul David, *The Indian Mutiny, 1857*, ch 3. But the more scholarly treatment of the sepoys' background recruitment and life in camp is in Seema Alavi, *The Sepoys and the Company: Tradition and Transition in Northern India, 1770–1830.*

[2]D. Butter, *Outline of the Topography and Statistics of the Southern Districts of Oudh*, 156.

[3]*Reorganization of the Indian Army: Papers Received from Col. Keith Young. Parliamentary Papers*, vol. viii (1859 session, part 2), 789.

[4]W.H. Sleeman, *A Journey through the Kingdom of Oude in 1849–50*, i, 170.

[5]W.H. Russell, *My Indian Mutiny Diary*, 227.

deserting non-commissioned officers and sepoys of the 22nd Native Infantry. This provides the names, castes, villages and parganas of 280 men. Of these only 5 per cent (fourteen men) came from districts that were not in Awadh. Of the remaining 266 men, 53 per cent (140 men) were from districts in southern Awadh or Baiswara.[6] This is a stray sample but it confirms the general impression that Awadh was the definitive recruiting ground of the Bengal Army. Therefore there is a strong probability that Mangal Pandey came from there.

One reason for the absence of records of recruitment before 1857 is the informal and haphazard way in which the sepoys were recruited. Sitaram Pandey joined as a sepoy and rose to the rank of subedar. He was loyal to the British during the revolt, although his son was a rebel. He wrote an autobiography the only one of its kind, which the British translated and publicised to hold Sitaram up as a model of good behaviour. The way in which Sitaram was brought into the army was fairly typical. He was the son of a small landholder in Tiloi in southern Awadh. His maternal uncle was a jemadar in the Bengal Native Infantry. On leave from his battalion, he would sit in the evenings in front of the house and relate to the family 'the wonders of the world he had seen, and the prosperity of the great Company Bahadur he served'. This fired young Sitaram's imagination, There was a monetary angle too. Young Sitaram was impressed by his uncle's 'unlimited supply of gold *mohurs*'. Sitaram's uncle told him that if he wanted to be a soldier then he (the uncle) would take him back to his regiment. Sitaram's father had other considerations in mind, as Sitaram recalled:

> There was a lawsuit impending over my father about his right to a mango grove of some 400 trees, and he thought that having a son in the Company Bahadur's service would be the means of getting his case attended in the law courts of Lucknow; for it was well known that a petition sent by a soldier through his commanding officer, who forwarded it onto the Resident sahib in Lucknow, generally had prompt attention paid to it, and carried more weight than even the bribes and party interests of a mere subject of the King of Oudh.[7]

[6]R. Mukherjee, *Awadh in Revolt, 1857–58*, 78.

[7]Sitaram, *From Sepoy to Subedar.* 4–5. Though Sitaram's autobiography is a remarkable and invaluable source for reconstructing the life of a sepoy in the Bengal Army, it should be pointed that doubts have been cast upon its authenticity. (See for example, J.A.B. Palmer, *The Mutiny Outbreak at Meerut in 1857*, 139:) These

There were many incentives to becoming a *sipahi* in the Company's army—glamour, a certain prestige, monetary gains and influence. Employment with the Company was thus an attractive proposition. This practice of recruiting soldiers from the peasantry was not a novelty that the British introduced. The kingdoms of Awadh and Benares also recruited their soldiers from the agricultural classes of the region. An active labour market existed in the Gangetic plain. The British tapped this source with greater efficiency and penetration, and offered more lucrative terms of employment. Moreover, once the British had subjugated or annexed the indigenous kingdoms, they became the most important source of employment for a particular group of people who had traditionally sought employment as sipahis.[8]

One consequence of recruiting from this labour market was the high-caste orientation of the sepoy army. The British were conscious of this and took steps to preserve it, and ensured that the religious sentiments of the high-caste sepoys were not hurt. In 1779, when reinforcements had to be sent from Bengal to Bombay to help in the first Anglo-Maratha War, Warren Hastings deliberately chose to send the sepoys by the slower overland route because he was aware that a sea voyage would result in the loss of caste for the high-caste sepoys as they would have travelled over the *kala pani*. It has been suggested that by promoting the high-caste orientation of its army, the British sought to legitimize their rule—having the high castes as their active collaborators furthered British legitimacy. Even if this is debatable, what is clear is that the Company's policy

---

doubts have been strengthened by the fact that the original Hindi manuscript has never been found. Neither has J.T. Norgate's original translation, which was apparently published in 1863, been located. The story of the original manuscript bears retelling. Sitaram was persuaded to pen the story of his life by Lt Col. Norgate. On completing the manuscript, Sitaram sent one copy to Norgate and he presented a second copy to the Bajpai family who were the landlords of Sitaram's village in Tiloi. The first extant edition was published from Lahore in 1873 and an Urdu translation followed. The second Hindi manuscript has disappeared even though Sir Girija Shankar Bajpai, perhaps India's most distinguished mandarin, recalled having read in 1915 the Hindi manuscript which had been given to his grandfather by Sitaram.

Neither Sir Girija's father nor his son, Uma Shankar, had any recollection of such a manuscript. The doubts also arise because it has been impossible to locate in which regiment Sitaram had served. See the Editorial Note to *From Sepoy to Subedar*.

[8]Alavi, *Sepoys and the Company*, chs 1 and 2.

of acknowledging and preserving the sepoys' caste status added to the attractiveness of the army as an employer.[9]

The sepoys thus carried bits of their rural life and customs into the regiment. The most important marker the sepoy carried from the village into the cantonment was caste. The daily routine of the Company's army in north India was tailored to accommodate the sepoys' caste requirements and taboos. The Company's military department made special arrangements for the sipahi' s diet so that his caste status was not compromised. Thus, Mangal Pandey and his fellow sepoys would have carried their own cooking utensils, cooked their own food and eaten alone. The place where they ate would be freshly smeared with cow dung to purify it. Dal and roti was the standard diet; meat, fish, alcohol, and even vegetables like potato, aubergine and radish were excluded. There was thus no common mess or communal kitchen—a normal feature of army life—for the sepoys of the English East India Company. The military department, moreover, granted the sepoy special time off to prepare his own food. The Company supplied the sepoys with only Brahmin and Rajput prostitutes.

Hindu festivals also became part of regimental life. By the General Order of 17 March 1793, the Commander-in-Chief allowed this so long as the celebration of the festivals was peaceful. Holi and Ramlila were popular and sometimes, much to the delight of the sepoys, the British officers also joined these celebrations. But the construction of temples was rarely allowed in the sepoy lines or in the cantonment. There was a deliberate attempt to build a kind of upper caste Hindu sanctuary within the army.[10] By doing this, the Company ensured the sepoys' loyalty and used them against other Indians when required. Such a strategy was a necessary condition of British rule in India in the first half of the 19th century.

Sepoys were peasants in uniform. But despite policies designed to preserve the high-caste character of the Bengal Army, a rigorous regime of discipline was imposed on the sepoy to make the peasant into a soldier. As long as he was on duty, the life of a sepoy was completely governed by the routines of regimental life. The bugle regulated his day, from the morning Reveille to the Last Post. His dress, his carriage, his gestures, his manner of standing when he

[9]Ibid., 44ff.

[10]The above is based on Alavi ch. 2.

was on parade, the holding of his head and so on were all parts of a prescribed and uniform pattern. Similarly, his verbal and physical gestures were routinized.

Being subject to the discipline of the army was the essential condition of military service. The army was the master of the sepoy's body, which was moulded into constant readiness. This created a contradiction of sorts. In his regimental life, the sepoy no longer behaved in a manner associated with peasant or rural life but in ways that had been drilled into him by the army. But the armour of military discipline had interstices, which provided space for the sepoy to retain some of his rural habits and the customs and traditions of his caste and religion.

The sepoy was not always completely comfortable with the discipline that he had to undergo. Sitaram remembered that he had found wearing the red coat 'very disagreeable'. He found it too tight under the arms. The shako, a tall headdress, he found was too heavy and it hurt his head.[11] When not on parade, the sepoys hardly ever wore their uniforms. As soon as they returned to their huts, they took off their tunics and trousers and lounged around in dhotis, as Mangal Pandey did on the afternoon of 29 March 1857, before he stormed onto the parade ground.

Breach of discipline resulted in punishments, which were inflicted directly on the sepoy's body. Flogging was the commonest form of punishment even though it was generally recognized to be degrading. Lord William Bentinck, Governor General from 1828 to 1832, was an advocate of the abolition of corporal punishment. But he was forced to concede that:

> ... there is a unanimous agreement in all the Committees, that this punishment, however degrading and injurious, cannot entirely be abolished ... With them all corporal punishment is the *sine qua non*, without which the discipline of the army cannot be maintained ... corporal punishment is venerated as the sole security against every military distemper, and as the, sole guarantee for the efficiency and good regulation of the army.[12]

The ultimate breach of discipline was mutiny, which is what Mangal Pandey's actions amounted to from the military point of view. The punishment for mutiny was invariably death. Hanging

[11]Sitaram, *Sepoy to Subedar.* 23.

[12]Quoted in R. Mukherjee, *Spectre of Violence: The 1857 Kanpur Massacres*, 40.

was the commonest mode of execution but sometimes to make the punishment exemplary another mode of execution was employed: blowing from the mouth of a cannon. An eyewitness to such an execution recorded that 'it was a most sickening sight ... the poor wretch was literally blown into atoms, the lookers-on being covered with blood, and fragments of flesh'.[13] A British officer who had actually carried out such an execution left behind the following account:

> The first man led out was a fine-looking young sepoy ... I had his wrists tied tightly, each to the upper part of a wheel of the gun. Then I depressed the muzzle, until it pointed to the pit of his stomach, just below the sternum ... Then I ordered the pot-fire to be lighted and gave the word 'Fire!' There was a considerable recoil from the gun, and a thick cloud of smoke hung over us. As this cleared away we saw two legs lying in front of the gun; but no other sign of what had just before, been a human being and a brave man. At this moment, perhaps from six to eight seconds after the explosion (and the same thing happened on the second occasion), down fell the man's head among us, slightly blackened but otherwise scarcely changed. It must have gone straight up into the air, probably about 200 feet ... I became aware that I was covered from head to foot, at least in front, with minute blackened particles of the man's flesh some of it sticking in my ears and hair.[14]

Sepoys were generally treated as inferior creatures by their white officers. One British resident in India wrote:

> The sepoy is [regarded as] an inferior creature. He is sworn at. He is treated roughly. He is spoken of as a 'nigger'. He is addressed as 'suar' or pig, an epithet most opprobrious to a respectable native, especially the Mussulman, and which cuts him to the quick. The old [officers] are less guilty ... But the younger men seem to regard it as an excellent joke, as an evidence of spirit and a praiseworthy sense of superiority over the sepoy to treat him as an inferior animal.[15]

The reference in the above passage to the older officers is important. A small but significant change had taken place in the

[13]R.M. Coopland, *A Lady's Escape from Gwalior*, 223.
[14]F.C. Maude, *Memories of the Mutiny*, i, 274.
[15]Quoted in Hibbert, *The Great Mutiny*, 56.

attitude of the white officers towards the sepoys. Sitaram was perceptive enough to note this.

> In those days [Sitaram wrote] the sahibs could speak our language much better than they do now, and they mixed more with us. Although officers today have to pass the language examination and have to read books, they do not understand our language ... The only language they learn is that of the lower orders, which they pick up from their servants, and which is unsuited to be used in polite conversation. The sahibs often used to give nautches for the regiment, and they attended all men's games. They also took us with them when they went out hunting ... Nowadays they seldom attend nautches because their padre sahibs have told them it is wrong. These padre sahibs have done and are still doing, many things to estrange the British officers from the sepoys. When I was a sepoy the captain of my company would have some of the men at his house all day long and he talked with them ... [most] of us went because we liked the sahib who always treated us as if we were his children ... I know that many officers nowadays only speak to their men when obliged to do so, and they show that the business is irksome and try to get rid of the sepoys as quickly as possible.[16]

In contrast to the 1850s, in the 1820s when Sitaram was a young sepoy. the colonel of the regiment was a familiar figure to his men. He was not just a disciplinarian but a father figure. He was well known even in the surrounding villages. A typical example was Major-General Hearsey, who charged at Mangal Pandey. Hearsey was fluent in Hindustani and his knowledge of Indian history, according to Lady Canning was 'prodigious'. The old-style officers referred to by Sitaram wrestled with their men, fenced with them and took them out hawking. These are recorded in the memoirs of officers of the time.[17] These officers, through the trust and loyalty that they won from the sepoys, served as important links to Indian society. One colonel, when on the march, used to send a sepoy ahead to find out who was the best chess player in the next village. Such officers, in the years immediately preceding 1857, were becoming figures of a bygone era. The typical British officer had become the 'pipe-clay rigid disciplinarian who would utterly extinguish the native in the soldier'.[18]

[16]Sitaram, *Sepoy to Subedar*, 24–25.
[17]See Hibbert, *The Great Mutiny*, 57 and 64;
[18]Ibid., 57.

And so we now have a general picture of Mangal Pandey's background, and the environment in which he served as a sepoy in the 34th Native Infantry. He possibly came from a village in Awadh or eastern UP and was brought to the army by some relative or kinsmen. He went through the drill that made him into a sepoy. There is nothing to suggest that before that fateful day, he was anything other than a typical sepoy in the Company's army. So what drove him to commit his extraordinary, indeed suicidal, act of defiance on that fateful Sunday in 1857?

CHAPTER THREE

The Greased Cartridge

When Mangal Pandey was exhorting his comrades to come out and join him, he spoke of how biting the cartridges would be a betrayal of their religion. The cartridges he was referring to were those of the Enfield Rifle which had recently been issued to the native soldiery. The matter of the greased cartridge has become the most cited cause of the mutiny of the sepoys in 1857. So much so that the last Mughal Emperor, who was more of a poet than a king, wrote according to legend:

Na Iran ne kiya, na Shah Russ ne—
Angrez ko tabah kiya kartoosh ne

(What Iran [i.e. the Crimean and Persian wars] and the Tsar of Russia could not do to the British, was achieved by the cartridge.)[1]

What was this cartridge and how did it come to acquire this importance?

In 1857, there were probably four types of firearms in use by the Indian soldiers of the infantry or cavalry regiments of the Bengal Army. First, there was a smooth-bore musket without any rifling. This was the Brown Bess which had been widely used in the Napoleonic wars and was the weapon in common use in the infantry regiments of the Bengal Army. But the faithful Brown Bess had undergone some modification: the percussion cap had replaced the flint as the igniter. Second, there was the Brunswick Rifle used by some of the native

[1]See J.A.B. Palmer, *The Mutiny Outbreak*, 7.

infantry regiments. This had two grooves of rifling. The third was an adoption of the Brunswick rifle, the Minie rifle, which was restricted in use. The distinctive feature of the Minie rifle was the structure of the bullet to which we shall turn in the next paragraph. Lastly, the cavalry used a shortened musket, which was known as a carbine.

The Minie rifle was named after a French officer who developed an elongated bullet with a metal thimble at the base that expanded when ignited. This solved certain problems regarding loading and firing that had previously existed but the metal thimble had a tendency to drive through the bullet. Experiments for further improvement were carried out at Enfield, which in 1853 evolved an improved form of bullet for use with a rifled weapon; which came to be known as the Enfield Rifle or more correctly as the Enfield-Pritchett rifle. (Pritchett was the man who invented the bullet). The ammunition for this was balled and was heavily greased at the base to facilitate loading. The standard practice for loading rifles was to bite the top off the cartridge and then pour the powder down the barrel. The rest of the cartridge, including the ball, was then put down the barrel with a ramrod. The grease on the Enfield cartridge became a matter of concern in India.[2]

One consideration was whether the grease would withstand the Indian climate. To test this, a consignment was sent out for sepoys to carry in their pouches. But the Commander-in-Chief of India (1850–56), General William Gomm, had warned about the grease and its implications for caste and religion in India. He had suggested that 'unless it be known that the grease employed in these cartridges is not of a nature to offend or interfere with the prejudices of caste, it will be expedient not to issue them for test to Native corps'. This warning was ignored, and after reports confirmed that the grease was not damaged by the weather in India, a shipment of greased cartridges and bullet moulds was sent out to India in 1856. After this cartridges began to be manufactured in the arsenals at Fort William, Meerut and Dum Dum. The components of the grease were the same as what had been used in the Royal Woolwich Arsenal—five parts tallow, five parts purified fatty acids and one part wax. The type of tallow being used was never specified.[3]

[2]The firearms in use in India in the 19th century are discussed in great technical detail in Palmer, *The Mutiny Outbreak*, 10ff and in a more accessible way in David, *Mutiny*, 52.

[3]This paragraph is based on David, *Mutiny*, 53.

In early January 1857, regiments of the Bengal Native Infantry were asked to send detachments to one of the three musketry depots in Dum Dum, Ambala or Sialkot. These detachments were to be trained and instructed to handle the new firearm and the new cartridge. It is important to underline that up to this point no sepoy had actually used the cartridge either in training or in the field. Some of them had only carried them around in 1855 in their pouches.

The presence of caste and its attendant rituals and prejudices in the sepoy lines has already been noted in the previous chapter. These now took over to provide an unexpected turn to events. It was reported that in the third week of January a low-caste khalasi who worked in the Dum Dum magazine asked a Brahmin sepoy for a drink of water from the latter's lota. The sepoy refused, saying that his lota would be defiled by the khalasi' s touch. The khalasi turned round and said, 'You will soon lose your caste, as ere long you will have to bite cartridges covered with the fat of pigs and cows.' The exact words of the khalasi are now lost. What is quoted here is the version recorded by Captain Wright, who commanded the Rifle Instruction Depot. General Hearsey was to give a slightly different version: 'The *saheb log* will make you bite cartridges soaked in cow and pork fat, and then where will your caste be?[4]

In his official report of the incident. Wright wrote the following:

> There appears to be a very unpleasant feeling existing among the native soldiers who are here for instruction, regarding the grease used in preparing the cartridges, some evil disposed persons having spread a report that it consists of a mixture of the fat of pigs and cows ... Some of the depot men, in conversing with me on the subject last night, said that the report had spread throughout India, and that when they go to their homes their friends will refuse to eat with them. I assured them (believing it to be the case) that the grease used is composed of mutton fat and wax; to which they replied, 'It may be so, but our friends will not believe it. Let us obtain the ingredients from the bazaar and make it up ourselves. We shall then know what is used, and be able to assure our fellow-soldiers and others that there is nothing in it prohibited by our caste'.[5]

[4]The incident in Dum Dum is well known. I have taken the version given in Palmer, *The Mutiny Outbreak*, 15.

[5]Quoted in Hibbert, *The Great Mutiny*, 63–64.

Hearsey, who received the report, agreed with the proposal that the sepoys should be allowed to grease cartridges with substances they found to be inoffensive. But the word and the fear had spread.

On 2 February, in Barrackpore, during the evening parade of the 2nd Native Infantry, the sepoys expressed their mistrust of the new cartridges and they now declared that they were suspicious of the cartridge paper as well. This meant that their fears about losing their caste would not disappear even if they used their own greasing material. In the court of inquiry that was instituted to investigate this kind of insubordinate behaviour, witness after witness spoke about their suspicions regarding the paper which they found to be very different from the old paper—'stiff and like cloth in the mode of tearing it' as one of the sepoys explained.[6]

On 6 February, while the court of inquiry was still meeting, a sepoy of the 34th Native Infantry stationed in Barrackpore approached Captain A.S. Allen in the evening in the latter's bungalow and requested a private audience. Once they were alone, the sepoy told Allen that a plot was being hatched among the four regiments in Barrackpore to rise up against their officers and burn their bungalows. This would be a protest against the attempts being made to despoil the sepoys' caste and religion and to make them Christians.[7] A jemadar from the same regiment also brought news of a conspiracy. He said two or three sepoys had approached him during the night and he had accompanied them to the parade-ground. There he found that 200 to 300 men had gathered. 'They had their heads tied up with cloths [the jemadar had reported] leaving only a small part of the face exposed. They asked me to join them, and I asked what was I to join them in. They replied that they were willing to die for their religion and that ... they would plunder the station and kill all the Europeans and go where they liked.'[8] From Ranigunj, 120 miles west from Calcutta, came news of incendiary fires aimed at a sergeant's bungalow and the destruction of the telegraph office. The troops stationed there were a wing of the 2nd Native Infantry (Grenadiers); the main body of this regiment was stationed in Barrackpore.[9] In Barrackpore too the telegraph

[6]*Selections*, i, 7–9.
[7]Ibid., 17.
[8]Ibid., 20.
[9]Palmer, *The Mutiny Outbreak*, 21.

office was attacked and bungalows set on fire.[10] The fear about the greased cartridge was spreading from sepoy to sepoy, from one sepoy line to another. To many in Barrackpore a mutiny seemed imminent. According to Hearsey, the situation in Barrackpore was a 'mine ready for explosion'.[11]

Hearsey decided to address the sepoys which he did on 9 February in fluent Hindustani. He wanted to impress upon the soldiers the absurdity of the notion that the government wanted to tamper with their caste and religion. The sepoys listened but there were no signs that they believed him. When the explosion did happen, it took place not in Barrackpore but in Berhampore, a small town 120 miles up the river from Calcutta.

On 11 February, a consignment of magazine stores was delivered from Dum Dum to the 19th Native Infantry at Berhampore. The stores included gunpowder and some practice cartridges. Two days later the authorities in Berhampore learnt that the 19th Native Infantry had received a *cossid* from 2nd Native Infantry (Grenadiers) asking for support in a rising. Lt Col. Mitchell, who was commanding the 19th, questioned the native officers about what reports they had heard about the new cartridges. They replied that the word was that the cartridges did contain beef and pork fat, but they themselves did not believe the story. This reassured Mitchell, who had implicit faith in the loyalty of the troops under him. He was mistaken in this. He ordered a parade on 27 February, and for the men to be issued with fifteen rounds of blank ammunition for the firing exercise. As per custom, the percussion caps were always distributed on the evening before the parade, during the sunset roll call. On 26 February, when the caps were distributed, the sepoys refused to take them, a sure sign that they would also refuse to take the cartridges the following morning. The senior non-commissioned officer, Subadar-Major Shaikh Murad Baksh, failed to convince his men that the cartridges were not contaminated. He called all the native officers and asked them to settle the matter with the troops before the roll call at 8.00 p.m. In the period between the two roll calls, it was later suggested, the sepoys had taken an oath not to take the cartridges and a small *panchayat* had even been held to coordinate the protest. Mitchell told his native officers to tell the sepoys that those who refused to take the cartridges would face

[10] Kaye, *Sepoy War*, i. 497.

[11] *Selections*, *i*, 24.

severe punishment. According to two native officers. Mitchell said that those who refused would be sent off to Burma and China where they would die of hunger and poverty. A number of sepoys heard Mitchell's threat. Mitchell further ordered the cavalry regiment to be present at the parade ground and instructed the Adjutant to post guns. There are no grounds to assume that the sepoys in the lines did not know of these orders even though they were issued in private.

A little before midnight, the officers of the 19th heard a commotion in the lines followed by the roll of drums. The sepoys had broken open the bell-of-arms and taken their weapons. Mitchell ordered the cavalry and the artillery out, and went with them to the parade-ground. He ordered the guns to load with grape and went down to his men. A discussion followed. The sepoys refused to give up their weapons unless the cavalry and artillery withdrew. Mitchell, on the advice of his native officers, was forced to agree to this. The sepoys then lodged their arms. The next night the sepoys slept around the bell-of-arms but did not break it open.[12] Bloodshed had been avoided, but only just.

A court of inquiry was ordered and this revealed some very significant points. All the witnesses were unanimous that the rumour about the cartridges had been circulating for two months at least. The taunt of the khalasi in Dum Dum may have been the first time the British had come to hear of it, but for the sepoys it had been a talking point for some time.[13] The evidence gathered suggests that the sepoys had acted not out of anger but out of fear. They had been alarmed by Mitchell's threats and they were convinced that the cavalry and the guns had been ordered to disarm them. The violence of the Colonel's harangue alarmed them and aggravated their suspicions about the cartridges. 'He gave this order so angrily,' the native officers wrote in their petition to the court of inquiry, 'that we were convinced that the cartridges were greased, otherwise he would not have spoken so.'[14]

The other point that the Berhampore émeute highlights is the extent of fraternising among the regiments. Throughout the month of February, various detachments of the 34th Native Infantry had come up to Berhampore from Barrackpore on some work or the

[12] I follow Palmer, *The Mutiny Outbreak*, 23–25 in my reconstruction of the Berhampore incident.

[13] Ibid., 26.

[14] Kaye, *Sepoy War*, i, 502n.

other. The sepoys of the two regiments, which had been stationed in Lucknow in the previous year during the annexation of Awadh, must have met and talked about their fears and even about their plans.

It is possible now to get some idea of what had stirred Mangal Pandey. He was by no means alone in his feelings. Barrackpore also seems to have been the centre of activity and disquiet. It is more than likely that Mangal Pandey. along with other sepoys, had attended some of the midnight meetings of the sepoys; that he knew who were responsible for the incendiary fires in Barrackpore; and that he was certainly alarmed by the proposed introduction of the new cartridges. He feared the loss of his caste and religion, and as the next chapter will show, the cartridges were not the only cause of his fears. His actions now have a context.

A POSTSCRIPT

Before leaving the matter of the greased cartridges, one question needs to be addressed, even though it has no direct bearing on the story of Mangal Pandey. Were the cartridges actually greased by beef and pork fat? No definite answer to this question is possible but there are pointers that are available. Lord Canning, the Governor General, stated in a letter dated 7 February 1857 that the fears regarding the grease had 'turned out to be well founded'. In March, the officer in charge of the Fort William arsenal admitted that no check had been carried out on the kind of fat that was being used for the cartridges. The inspector-general of Ordnance, Colonel Augustus Abbott, reported that the tallow that had been used could 'have contained the fat of cows or other animals'.[15] The sepoys thus had grounds for suspicion. But grease had been used by the sepoys before without any objections from them. What was there in 1857 that made them apprehensive about the government's intentions?

[15]David, *Mutiny*, 54–55.

CHAPTER FOUR

Chapati, Rumours and Prophecy

The British in 1857, and subsequent historians of the revolt, have failed to explain how the rumour about the greased cartridges originated. There were other phenomena observed in the beginning of 1857 whose origins and meaning remain mysteries even to this day. The best known of these is the circulation of chapatis.

The first report of this mysterious phenomenon came from the environs of Delhi in February–March. The British officer who took note of it reported that:

> ... a signal has passed through numbers of the villages of this district, the purport of which has not yet transpired. The Chowkeydars [watchmen] of the villages bordering on those belonging to Mutra have received small baked cakes of atta with orders to distribute them generally through this district. A Chowkeydar, upon receiving one of these cakes, has had five or six more prepared, and thus they have passed from village to village; so quickly has the order been executed that village after village has been served with the notice.[1]

Similar reports came from other districts from north India from where bewildered British officers sent accounts of how swiftly the chapatis circulated. The chapatis, one officer recorded, 'travelled often over 160 or 200 miles in a night'.[2] The reports seldom varied except in detail. W.G. Erskine, the commissioner of the Sagar and Narmada territories, summed up the strange occurrences thus:

[1]Kaye, *Sepoy War*, i, 632.

[2]Quoted in Palmer, *The Mutiny Outbreak*, I

> So far back as January 1857 small wheaten cakes (chupatties) were passed in a most mysterious manner from village to village in most of the districts, and although all took it as a signal that something was coming nobody in the division, I believe, knew what it portended, or whence it came ... I reported the matter to Government at the time, but even now it is a matter of doubt if the signal was understood by *anyone*, or if it referred to the coming rebellion, though such is now the general opinion.[3]

Even today, nearly 150 years after the event, nobody quite knows what the chapatis symbolized or signified.

The interpretation that sees it as a signal for the outbreak is a post facto linking of two distinct phenomena; because it occurred immediately prior to the uprising, it was assumed that it was a signal for the conflagaration. One could say, here was a clear case of the logical fallacy of *post hoc, ergo propter hoc* (after this, so because of this: the fallacy of arguing that because one event happened after another, it happened because of it). There was nothing in the circulation of chapatis to suggest that a conflagration was coming. The circulation of objects to prevent the occurrence of an epidemic was common in parts of north India but this does not warrant the conclusion that the chapatis prefigured an uprising against the British.[4] Ranajit Guha's concluding remarks on the subject are worth quoting:

> The symbolic agent of an epidemic in the countryside it took on an added meaning as the carrier of an imminent but undefined political holocaust. No index of any kind of conspiracy, it connected neither with the past nor with the present. As an omen it looked ahead of events, and in an atmosphere charged with growing unrest in agrarian communities and army barracks it transmitted the rebellion in anticipation by sounding a tocsin for all to hear but none yet to understand why.

What was it that so charged the atmosphere that it added an excess of meaning to the circulation of chapatis? Chapatis were not the only things that went around north India in the early months of 1857. It was also the season for rumours in north India and they went around thick and fast. Almost all of them related to a deliberate design of the British to tamper with the caste and religion of the

[3]Kaye, *Sepoy War*, i, 573n.

[4]See the discussion on the circulation of chapatis in Ranajit Guha, *Elementary Aspects of Peasant Insurgency in Colonial India*, 239–46.

sepoys and other Indians. According to one rumour, the British had mixed the bone-dust of cows and pigs with the attah that was sold in the bazaar. One British officer stationed in Lucknow noted the phenomenon in some detail:

> Government, it was said, had sent up cartloads and boatloads of bone-dust, which was to be mixed up with the flour and sweetmeats sold in the bazaar, whereby the whole population would lose their caste. The public mind became greatly excited. On one day in Sultanpoor, it was spread over the station that a boat had arrived at a certain ghaut on the river Goomtee laden with bone-dust, and the sepoys were hardly restrained from outbreak. A few days later at the station in Salone, two camels laden with ammunition, arrived at the house of Captain Thompson the commandant. It was rumoured that the packages contained bone-dust and a panic spread through the station. Not only the sepoys in their lines, but the domestic servants about the officers' bungalows, and the villagers and zemindars attending court hastily flung away. untasted, the food which they had cooked, and fasted for the day. At Lucknow, the *rumours* which were whispered about were perpetual, and the public mind was never allowed to rest. Now it was at one shop, the next day in another bazaar, that despatches of bone-dust had, it *was asserted*, been received. It was in vain that facts were opposed to this prevailing panic.[5]

Rumours about pollution created an atmosphere of alarm and suspicion. Articles of everyday consumption were said to have been tampered with—salt, sugar, wheat, ghee and even water. It was rumoured that *once* Hindus and Muslims consumed these contaminated items, they would lose their religion and then they would be converted to become Christians. Persuasion and reassurance by the sahibs were of no avail. The Company Bahadur and its officers could no longer be trusted. Henry Lawrence, the chief commissioner of Awadh, was taken aback by the dogged belief of a jemadar in the Awadh artillery—a man of excellent character, according to Lawrence—that for the last ten years the government had been 'engaged in measures for the forcible or rather fraudulent conversion of all natives'.[6] In the context of these rumours, it is

[5]M.R. Gubbins, *An Account of the Mutinies in Oudh and the Siege of the Lucknow Residency*, 86.

[6]Henry Lawrence to Canning, 9 May 1857, quoted in H.B. Edwardes and M. Merivale, *Life of Sir Henry Lawrence*, ii, 322.

easy to comprehend how the story of the greased cartridges caught on and how chapatis became a tocsin. These became talking points in the sepoy lines. Here, the rural origins of the sepoys acquire significance. Since the rumours touched the two most sensitive aspects of men's lives in the 19th century—caste and religion—the alarm and suspicion of the sepoys in the lines were quickly passed on to the villages; and what was heard in the *mulk* came back to the lines.

Nobody knew how the rumours originated. They were also unverifiable. Moreover, facts had become irrelevant, what was important was what the people believed and how they reacted out of that belief. Here suspicion and alarm prevailed. One thing is worth noting: rumours circulated most in bazaars where people gathered. 'The lies of the bazaar,' Kaye called them.[7] Rumours touched on issues that lay deep in Indian sentiments. With the rumours circulated a prophecy: British rule would end on the centenary of the battle of Plassey. Sitaram recalled: 'Our learned men ... told us that the Company's rule would come to an end in 1857, since this was one hundred years after the Company's first great battle.'[8] Rumours and prophecy merged together and moved men's minds and stirred them to action.

It is reasonable to assume that Mangal Pandey had heard of the prophecy and had encountered the rumours; and that he shared the fear and terror that the rumours spread. He was an ordinary sepoy and, like his comrades, he too feared the loss of his caste and religion, he too must have discussed the rumours, their implications and must have contemplated the possibility of contamination through food and greased cartridges. He may have wondered what the chapatis signified as the news of their circulation came in from north India. It is possible that, in ways that we cannot fathom today, the chapatis did signify something to him and other sepoys.

There is one remarkable document that vividly conveys the state of mind of Mangal Pandey and other sepoys in Barrackpore in 1857. This was an anonymous petition sent to Major Matthews, who comnanded the 43rd regiment in Barrackpore. It was picked up 'at the gate of Major Matthews' in March 1857. Kaye noted that it was the earliest in date of documents of a similar nature. The document records what Indians, especially sepoys, suspected the British of planning and doing. Here is an extract from the petition:

[7]Kaye, *Sepoy War*, i. 492.
[8]Sitaram, *Sepoy to Subedar*, 173.

> The representation of the whole station is this, that we will not give up our religion. We serve for honour and religion; if we lose our religion the Hindoo and Mahomedan religions will be destroyed ... You are the masters of the country. The Lord Sahib has given orders, which he has received from the Company, to all commanding officers to destroy the religion of the country. We know this, as all things are being bought up by Government. The officers of the Salt Department mix up bones with the salt. The officer in charge of the ghee mixes up fat with it; this is well known. These are two matters. The third is this: that the Sahib in charge of the sugar burns up bones and mixes them in the syrup the sugar is made of; this is well known-all know it. The fourth is this: that in the country the Burra Sahibs have ordered the Rajahs, Thakurs, Zemindars, Mahajans and Ryots, all to eat together, and English bread has been sent to them; this is well known. And this is another affair, that throughout the country the wives of respectable men, in fact, all classes of Hindoos, on becoming widows, are to be married again; this is known. Therefore we consider ourselves as killed ... A king, or any other one who acts unjustly, does not remain. With reference to the sepoys, they are your servants; but to destroy their caste, a council assembled and decided to give them muskets and cartridges made up with greased paper to bite; this is also evident. We wish to represent this to the General, that we do not approve of the new musket and cartridge; the sepoys cannot use them. *You* are the masters of the country: if you will give us our discharge we will go away. [9]

Mangal Pandey's immediate environment in Barrackpore was thus agog with accounts of British designs to despoil the caste and religion of the Indians. The petition appears to be a collective expression on the part of the entire station and the sepoys claim to be authors of the document. It is possible that this appeal grew out of the midnight meetings, reports of which had already come to British officers. Mangal Pandey was one of a collective. His outburst on 29 March was an individual act, but it grew out of a collective anger and a collective sense of desperation and helplessness. The sepoys, as the petition said, were willing to be discharged and to go back to their villages. Loss of livelihood was preferable to the loss of caste and religion. Witnesses testified, and Mangal Pandey himself admitted during his trial, that he had been under the influence of bhang on the afternoon of 29 March. But he was not so drugged as to be in a stupor. On the contrary, he was in a state of high excitement. Even

[9]Quoted in Kaye, *Sepoy War*, i.639–41.

in that state, Mangal Pandey could not have been unaware of the consequences of what he had set out to do. Indeed, it will not be at all illogical to suggest that he had taken bhang to give him courage by making him forget the consequences. The intoxicant probably facilitated his show of defiance.

Any description of what happened in Barrackpore reveals that Mangal Pandey's lone act of defiance had an undercurrent of support from some of the sepoys who had gathered in the parade ground that afternoon.

There is first the jemadar's excuse that he could not arrest Mangal Pandey because the havildar and the naik had gone on errands and that he could not possibly take Mangal Pandey alone. The guard grumbled when ordered to load by Hewson and then refused to follow his orders. When Hewson and Baugh advanced upon Mangal Pandey, according to Hewson's recollection of events, the former was struck by rifle butts from behind. Wheler's orders to advance upon Mangal Pandey were defied by the guard who only took a few steps forward and then stopped. And finally, Hearsey was told by the sepoys that they had not attacked Mangal Pandey as his musket was loaded. That afternoon, no other sepoy, save Sheikh Paltu, came forward to restrain Mangal Pandey and to protect the British officers. Sheikh Paltu was threatened with death by the sepoys if he continued to hold on to Mangal Pandey.

Mangal Pandey was the only sepoy to take up arms against the British but there were other sepoys that afternoon who had expressed their defiance and insubordination on different, though minor, scales. There was a definite show of solidarity for Mangal Pandey. The latter's actions grew out of a collective misgiving. In this context, what Mangal Pandey had to say in his trial assumes a certain salience.

CHAPTER FIVE

The Trial

Mangal Pandey was tried in Barrackpore on 6 April 1857. The verdict was a foregone conclusion and he was hanged two days later. The jemadar, Iswaree Pandey, who had commanded the quarter-guard and had not arrested Mangal Pandey, was also executed a few days later.[1]

The trial was not an elaborate affair. The persons concerned—Hewson, Baugh, Hearsey, Sheikh Paltu and some others—gave evidence. Their testimonies form the basis on which historians reconstruct any narrative of events of 29 March 1857. After each person's testimony, Mangal Pandey was asked if he had anything to say or ask. He declined each time.

The court asked him if he was under the influence of any drugs. He answered that of late he had been taking bhang and opium and added, 'I was not aware at the time of what I was doing.' He had very little to say for himself. His responses had two refrains. One was that he did not know what he was doing when he had acted as he had been intoxicated, and the other was that he had acted completely on his own and had no accomplices. 'Did you act on Sunday last by your own free will, or were you instructed by others?' he was asked. He replied, 'Of my own free will.' He was asked again and again to provide the names of persons who, as he himself had cried on that afternoon, had incited him. He refused to do so. When called upon for his defence, he fell back on what he had said a number

[1]There is a very dramatic retelling of Mangal Pandey's trial in Bengali by Sripantha (Nikhil Sarkar) in *Mangal Pandeyer Bichar.*

of times earlier: 'I did not know what I was doing. I did not know who I wounded and who I did not. What more shall I say? I have nothing more to say. I have no evidence.'[2]

The only thing of importance that was learnt in the trial was that Mangal Pandey was twenty-six years old and had been a sepoy of the Bengal Army for seven years. His conduct had always been good and until 29 March there was no charge against him of any misbehaviour to sully his record. In the previous chapters, we have made an attempt to present the context that set Mangal Pandey on the course of action that broke, fatally and significantly, his record of good behaviour. It was this transgression that catapulted him from anonymity and obscurity and into the pages of history.

But a context is not an explanation. We still do not know what made Mangal Pandey act the way he did. The context was operative for all the sepoys in Barrackpore but only one individual acted; the others merely watched, though some may have tacitly encouraged him. But it was that individual act that entered history, and it is this act that cries out for an explanation. It is here that the historian hits a wall. There is nothing in the historical records that helps to understand Mangal Pandey's actions unless one accepts that he broke rank and discipline under the influence of bhang. The records of the court martial of Mangal Pandey are the obvious place to look for clues to an explanation. But the records yield nothing as the principal actor refused to speak. The proceedings of the court had offered Mangal Pandey an opportunity to speak to history. He had turned down that opportunity.

What are we to make of this trial, especially of the steadfast silence that Mangal Pandey maintained? In one sense, the trial was a show, since the outcome was predetermined. There was not a ghost of a chance that Mangal Pandey would escape the death sentence. The British rewarded loyalty—Sheikh Paltu was promoted even before Mangal Pandey went to the gallows—and came down with severity on any show of defiance and insubordination on the part of sepoys. An armed assault on a white officer deserved nothing less than death. To do otherwise would be to set a bad example, to show weakness and encourage recalcitrant behaviour. The court martial thus only went through the motions of gathering evidence for the record. It was as part of the procedure of the trial that the accused was given the chance to speak or even to cross-examine. But

[2]*Selections*, i, 52.

even this was a bit of a charade. What could an illiterate sepoy, who came most probably from rural Awadh, ask in a trial? He probably did not understand all that was going on around him. He was also in all probability cowed down by fear as the realization of what he had perpetrated dawned on him. In a trial, a sepoy was always in a helpless situation. The Mutiny Act was read out to him in Persian and Arabic rather than in the vernacular language of the sepoy. Language problems plagued military tribunals and sepoys were often denied the services of accurate and unbiased translations.[3]

If Mangal Pandey had decided to speak, he could have lightened his guilt naming others who may have been implicated. He could have spoken about the midnight meetings, identified the sepoys who had been hanging around and those who had hit Hewson from behind. He could have explained why he had said on that afternoon that he had been incited by other sepoys who were refusing to join him. He could have also spoken of his fears about the greased cartridge and the loss of caste and religion. Was his silence a show of solidarity or a show of helplessness? It is significant that the court martial did not offer to him the characteristic approver's reward. He was not told that if he identified his accomplices his sentence would be lightened. He chose to be silent because he knew that, one way or another, his own death was certain. His show of solidarity—if solidarity it was—was determined by his circumstances. What would he gain by speaking? What was the point of making some of his brothers-in-arms suffer the fate that most certainly awaited him? There is no evidence to justify the view that this sepoy was a martyr and hero who decided to die with honour, betraying none of his coconspirators, and expressing no regret or remorse.

But this is precisely the status that has been endowed on Mangal Pandey by nationalists in India. V.D. Savarkar hailed him as shahid, as the man who started it all—the first rebel of 1857 who lit the spark.[4] He is placed in the Valhalla of martyrs who died for their motherland and freedom. Nationalism everywhere makes its own myths, and Mangal Pandey has become part of that imagination. Clio, where she clearly and self-consciously, demarcates her own terrain from Mythos, has to distance herself from that imagination.

[3]See Douglas M. Peers, 'Sepoys, Soldiers and the Lash: Race, Caste and Army Discipline in India, 1820–1850' in *The Journal of Imperial and Commonwealth History*, vol. 23 (1995). 225.

[4]V.D. Savarkar, *The Indian War of Independence, 1857*, 101–06.

Mangal Pandey had no notion of patriotism or even of India. For him mulk was his small village in Awadh; his *watan*, a small plot of land that his father and forefathers cultivated. To bestow patriotism on him is to wrench him away from his own time and context. If love for his country drove him he would not have become a sepoy in the first place.

Mangal Pandey also had no idea that he was starting something. Indeed, did he start anything? The revolt began only on 10 May, nearly one month after he had been hanged, and that too not in Barrackpore but far away in Meerut. The sepoys in Meerut, as they killed the *firanghi* looted the treasury, broke open the jail and cut the telegraph wires, did not look towards Mangal Pandey, if they knew of him at all. They looked towards Delhi and the Mughal Emperor. Mangal Pandey cannot be endowed with telos since it is not possible to suggest with any certitude that his actions were in anyway linked with the events that engulfed north India in the summer of 1857.

Indeed, in one crucial way, Mangal Pandey's action was somewhat contrary to the spirit of insurgency. A rebellion's real strength lies in the collective. A rebellion represents a collective will to overthrow an oppressive order. Mangal Pandey's action was that of an individual. His defiance may have been grounded in a collective sense of fear, suspicion and anger but its manifestation was individualistic. At the critical juncture the collective anger and fear did not translate into direct action. Mangal Pandey acted alone. He was a rebel without a rebellion. The rebellion, when it came more than a month later, left Barrackpore untouched and did not claim Mangal Pandey as the sepoy who began it all. That status fell on him when historians began writing narratives of the uprising. Kaye described Mangal Pandey as a fugleman.[5]

The execution of Mangal Pandey was not the last episode in the drama that had begun in Barrackpore at the end of March. The 19th Native Infantry that had mutinied in Berhampore was marched down to Barrackpore. The day after Mangal Pandey's attack on the white officers, the regiment had reached Barasat, where, according to reports, it was met by members of the 34th Native Infantry, Mangal Pandey's regiment. The latter wanted the 19th to join them in mutiny. The plan did not work because the sepoys of the 19th were not willing. They marched on to Barrackpore, and a mile outside the

[5]Kaye, *Sepoy War*, i, 543.

cantonment they were met by Hearsey. The general placed himself at the head of the column and marched them into the parade ground. There, surrounded by all the troops of the Presidency Division, British and native and facing guns, they were disbanded.[6] The 19th offered no resistance to this degradation. Disbanding a regiment or discharging an individual sepoy was public humiliation since it directly affected the sepoy's or the regiment's honour and status.[7] The disbandment of the 19th was replicated for the 34th a few weeks later. It was thought that the 34th was too deeply implicated in the events of 29 March to be trusted any longer. The regiment was disarmed and disbanded on 21 April. The sepoys of the 34th were not as quiet and submissive as their brothers in the 19th Native Infantry. They threw their caps on the ground and trampled on them before leaving the parade ground. Their looks 'suggested they would cause further trouble when they could'.[8]

The trampling of the caps was symbolic of the severance of their last ties with the British army. It was more obviously a show of anger and disappointment. The sepoys' disappointment sprang from the lack of sympathy and understanding from the British officers. The sepoys expected their superior officers, men like Hearsey for example, to empathise with their plight. What was most dear to the sepoys was under threat. The sepoys felt that the Company's policies were placing their religion and caste under a shadow. This was the perception—the truth of the matter was of no consequence in such an issue. Back in the villages, the sepoys and their families would be ostracized and would lose their caste status. The sepoys expected the colonel sahib or the major sahib to understand this. When the sepoys were driven to defiance or even to conspiracy, it was because they wanted to protect their dharma. This was more important to them than the army discipline and their livelihood. British officers, or most of them at any rate, refused to listen to the sepoys, let alone understand their despair. There was a gap in communication and a clash of values. Moreover, as some authorities had noted as early as 1820, the sepoys did not look upon the crime of treason against the state in the same light as the British did.[9] The British failure to get across their values and their authority to the sepoys is an index

[6]Ibid., 544–55.

[7]See Peers, 'Sepoys. Soldiers and the Lash', 229–30.

[8]Hibbert, *The Great Mutiny*, 71–72.

[9]Peers, 'Sepoys, Soldiers and the Lash', 225.

of the incompleteness of their rule and sovereignty. British rule was always, as Ranajit Guha has so tellingly noted, 'dominance without hegemony'.[10] Barrackpore played out in microcosm some of the most noted features of the uprising of 1857: defiance, bloodshed and retribution. But during the actual uprising, when all the three elements, magnified many times over, became visible every day across the Gangetic plain through the summer, autumn and winter of 1857, Barrackpore remained quiet and neighbouring Calcutta, the capital of the Raj, utterly loyal.[11]

[10]R. Guha, 'Colonialism in South Asia: A Dominance Without Hegemony and it's Historiography' in *Dominance Without Hegemony: History and Power in Colonial India*, 1–99.

[11]The loyalty of the Calcutta western-educated literati is well documented. It is captured with biting satire in *Hootum Pyanchar Naksha* (1862) by Kaliprasanna Sinha. This loyalty was ridiculed by the British, *The Englishman* (26 May 1857) lampooned them thus:

March, march, baboos of Calcutta
Let us offer our aid with the choicest Soft Sawder
March to the meeting though each heart may flutter.
To think that black baboos are bound into
Keep Order.
Paunchy old Toolsee Doss
Fat, flabby Ramdhone Ghose
Come to the meeting and offer assistance.
Neither Dutt, Seal and Sen
Come now, but don't come when
There seems to be the least chance of resistance.

Quoted in P.C. Gupta, *Nana Sahib and the Rising at Cawnpore*, 122.

CHAPTER SIX

Epilogue

The previous chapter suggested that Mangal Pandey's actions, despite what Kaye and Savarkar had claimed from different perspectives, had little or no impact and influence on what happened in north India in the months of May and June the same year. It is significant that in April a group of sepoys had said in Kanpur, according to a resident of the place, that 'we shall quarrel with Government presently; for new cartridges prepared with cows' and pigs' fat are going to be served out, and the sepoys refuse to receive them'. These sepoys the British identified as 'the disbanded men of the 19th Regiment Native Infantry from Barrackpore'.[1] But the sepoys from Barrackpore—and it is unlikely that when they spoke to their comrades in Kanpur and in other sepoy lines that dotted the Gangetic plain, they would not have spoken of what Mangal Pandey had done—could not incite or provoke a single mutiny in any of the regiments stationed in north India. It was the news of the mutiny in Meerut, and of the fall of Delhi to the mutineers, that lit the flame of insurgency all over north India. As one officer put it:

> ... the intelligence received of the mutiny of the troops at Meerut appears to have lit the flame at Cawnpore, as well as at every other station it reached. So daring an act of mutiny with murder of their Officers in the presence of an overwhelming European force—the repetition in Delhi—the seizure of the City with the proclamation of a rebel king, encouraged and strengthened the hands of the

[1]See Mukherjee, *Spectre of Violence*, 47.

disaffected amongst the native troops and other classes in the station and neighbourhood.[2]

To answer the puzzle about why Meerut acted as a kind of trigger and not Mangal Pandey, it is necessary to quickly summarize what happened in Meerut.[3] On 24 April, the skirmishers of the 3rd Light Cavalry were ordered to attend a parade where they would be taught the new firing drill. The sepoys refused to touch the cartridges unless all other regiments agreed to handle them. The sepoys were informed that these were not the new cartridges but they stood steadfast in their resolve. They had in fact sworn—the Muslims on the Koran and the Hindus on the Ganges—that they would not touch the cartridges which they had been told were greased with the fat of pigs and cows. The European officers had been warned about this refusal but Colonel George Monro Carmichael-Smyth chose not to heed the warnings and went ahead with the parade.

During the parade all eighty-five sepoys refused to take the cartridges and each of them said that he would get a bad name if he did take them. They were all confined to the lines. A court of inquiry was instituted and following its findings, a court martial instituted. The sepoys were convicted and sentenced to ten years of rigorous imprisonment. The sentence was carried out on 9 May in the presence of all the troops of Meerut. As was usual, the sentence was executed as a spectacle. The troops formed three sides of a square and on the open side the convicted sepoys marched in and halted. The European regiments were all fully armed, their guns and rifles loaded. The eighty-five men were stripped of their uniforms; their boots removed and ankles shackled. Many of the sepoys cursed the colonel, threatened reprisals and asked the gathered sepoys to rescue them. The 'convicts'—they had lost their sepoy status in the eyes of the British—were then marched off under a guard to the jail.

That same evening, Lt Hugh Gough of the 3rd Light Cavalry, was visited by a native officer of the regiment when the lieutenant was relaxing in the veranda of his bungalow. The native officer informed Gough that the next day, the sepoys of Meerut would mutiny. Gough took the report seriously as he was aware that since the arrest of the eighty-five sepoys, parts of Meerut had witnessed acts of arson

[2]Ibid.

[3]The most detailed account of the mutiny in Meerut is Palmer, *The Mutiny Outbreak;* also see Hibbert, *The Great Mutiny*, 75–90 and David, *Mutiny*, ch. 8.

and that in the bazaar a high level of tension prevailed. Gough did his duty by reporting what he had been told to his Colonel, who treated the information with contempt. Officers higher up in the hierarchy, the Brigadier and the Major-General commanding the Meerut division, were also incredulous.

Sunday, 10 May, began like any other Sunday in Meerut: the sahibs and the memsahibs attended church. It was a very hot day, so hot that the evening church parade had been postponed by half an hour to seven o'clock. But that parade was not destined to be held. By six o'clock, British officers, sitting in their bungalows, heard the sounds of guns being fired and saw smoke enveloping the evening sky. Some bungalows were already on fire. The sepoys were in uproar: some regiments had already captured the bells of arms and had seized the weapons; the 11th Native Infantry had killed its Colonel; the mutiny had begun. The sepoys ransacked and looted European and government property and shot every single European, irrespective of gender and age, in sight. The sepoys were joined by civilians from the towns and the neighbouring villages. Already, in its very initial moments, the mutiny was beginning to acquire features of a general uprising. Two actions of the sepoys in the collective frenzy needs to be highlighted. The first was the attack on the jail to free the sepoys who had been imprisoned there the previous day. And second was when a group of them, having first cut the telegraph wires, decided to march to Delhi to carry the news of the uprising to the Mughal capital.

May in 1857 was the Muslim holy month of Ramzan. The Mughal Emperor, Bahadur Shah II, eighty-two years old, had begun his fast when the sepoys from Meerut arrived at his door in the Lal Qila. The sepoys' appeal to the monarch was simple: they said they were fighting for their faith and wanted the emperor's support and leadership. The emperor was in no position to respond and the sepoys entered the city. Inside the city, they got a different kind of response. The sepoys in Delhi joined them as did the ordinary people. Collectively, they killed Europeans and destroyed and looted their property. By 12 May, the British had lost control of Delhi. What was equally important was that Bahadur Shah, under pressure from the insurgent population all around him in Delhi, had accepted the leadership of the mutiny that was poised to become a rebellion.

Historians are prone to establishing a relationship between sequence and consequence: the significance of the fall of Delhi is clear from its sequel. No regiment in north India mutinied immediately after the events of Meerut. It was only after Delhi had fallen and the news of this event had begun to travel that the regiments raised the banner of revolt. Noting this, I wrote in a previous book: 'The dates of the mutinies seem to indicate a pattern: 20 May, Aligarh, 23 May, Etawah and Mainpuri and 27 May, Etah. It was as if the mutinies were traveling down the Ganges valley from Meerut and Delhi, with a time-gap between the various stations required for the news to travel from one place to another.'[4] Kaye wrote, 'At this time [after the fall of Delhi] news was traveling through the country.[5] Every single cantonment saw a replication of what had happened in Meerut and Delhi: killing of the firanghi, destruction of their property, attack on government offices and on people perceived to be allies of the British. By June, British rule was non-existent in north India, with the surviving Britons cowering within the walls of the Lucknow Residency, behind Wheeler's 'entrenchment' in Kanpur and on the Ridge in Delhi. British rule in north India, one officer noted, had collapsed 'like a house made of cards'.[6]

The mutinous sepoys of north India did not look towards Calcutta or Barrackpore but towards Delhi. If the actions of Mangal Pandey had been their inspiration, they did not articulate it. Statements by rebellious sepoys are not many, but those that exist do not speak of Mangal Pandey and Barrackpore. The same issues that had stirred Mangal Pandey—loss of caste, fears about religion, the greased cartridge—had spurred the sepoys in Meerut and in other stations in the Gangetic plain. Other than this, there is no evidence to suggest any links between Mangal Pandey's fateful action and the mutinies in north India. On the basis of the available evidence, it would not be an exaggeration, nor would it be unjustified, to assert that the name Mangal Pandey meant nothing to the sepoys who raised the flag of revolt in 1857.

But Mangal Pandey was a name that haunted the British, especially as they found that Pandey was a common surname among the Brahmin sepoys recruited from Awadh. In a metonymic slide, Pandey became a synonym for mutineer. The myth that surrounds the name of Mangal Pandey is a British creation. The putative first

[4]Mukherjee, *Awadh in Revolt*, 65–66.

[5]Kaye, *Sepoy War*, iii, 432.

[6]M.R. Gubbins, *An Account of the Mutinies*, 118.

hero of Indian nationalism is a British reconstruction. Heroism, one could say, slightly altering T.S. Eliot, often has unnatural fathers. A revolt, which by definition is a product of a collective agency, cannot have a single inaugurator. Mangal Pandey, when he shot at his British officer could not have known what was going to happen in Meerut and the rest of north India a month after he walked to the gallows. Later historians have linked his name to events that came after him, which in all probability were unconnected to his act of defiance.

Yet this analysis leaves out certain aspects of Mangal Pandey's actions. In his show of defiance at the parade ground that March afternoon, Mangal Pandey had made gestures towards a collective agency. There was his call to his comrades who he said had incited him to come out and defy. There was his call to save caste and religion. Behind these cries lurk the midnight torch-lit meetings of sepoys which were reported later during the enquiry. In his sullen refusal to speak during his trial, one can detect a gesture of solidarity to a collective he chose not to identify. The collective was thus elusive. There are signs of its presence but it is impossible to identify. It was a collective that refused to come out in the open and claim for itself the authorship of a rebellion. For such a claim to emerge, the locus had to shift from Barrackpore to Meerut, and the articulation to a different register—from individual defiance to open and collective rebellion.[7]

The shadow that subsequent history throws on the representation of an event is clear from what happened in the course of another mutiny in Barrackpore some thirty-three years before Mangal Pandey decided to attack his white officers. In 1824, in the first two days of November, the sepoys in Barrackpore mutinied. To suppress the mutiny, 200 sepoys were killed by the Royal Artillery on the parade ground and twelve more hanged.[8] This was obviously a show of resistance much fiercer than what happened in March 1857 on the same parade ground. In contrast to what Mangal Pandey did, the 1824 mutiny was much more open and collective. Yet this insurgent moment has never received the kind of attention that Pandey's

[7]For the importance of collectivity and openness in rebellion, see Guha, *Elementary Aspects*, chs 3 and 4.

[8]The only detailed study of the 1824 mutiny is P.K. Bandyopadhyay, *Tulsi Leaves and the Ganges Water: The Slogan of the First Sepoy Mutiny in Barrackpore* (Kolkata, 2003). All facts regarding the 1824 mutiny are taken from this study.

individualistic action did. This is explained by the fact that the 1824 mutiny had no intended or unintended aftermath. It remained an isolated act of mutiny on the part of some sepoys belonging to three Native Infantry regiments—the 26th, 47th and 62nd. The sepoys refused to board the ships to go and fight in Burma, as they believed travelling across the kala pani would result in a loss of caste. The mutiny was preceded by meetings of the sepoys. It was brutally crushed by the Royal Artillery which opened fire on the sepoys.

There is no available evidence that this mutiny had any impact on sepoys in the stations of north India but in October 1825, in Rungpore in Assam, the sepoys of the 46th Native Infantry, having heard of the Barrackpore mutiny from some fellow sepoys, also mutinied, urging their comrades not to march to Burma. To mobilize the sepoys unsigned handwritten pamphlets were circulated. Thus, like Mangal Pandey in 1857, the sepoys in Barrackpore and Rungpore in 1824–25 were driven to mutiny because they feared the loss of their caste.

The mutinies of 1824–25 have never received the kind of attention that Mangal Pandey's actions have received. In fact, the first full-scale study of those mutinies appeared only in 2003. By any reckoning, the 1824–25 mutinies were more substantial as acts of protest and resistance and constituted a bigger threat to the British than one sepoy's act of defiance, which is what Mangal Pandey's action represented. The reason for the attention given to Mangal Pandey lies not in the significance of his own actions but in the actions of the sepoys of north India who took to arms in the summer of 1857. Historians have assumed a link between Mangal Pandey and the uprising of 1857 and thus a legend has been created around his name.

History writing has an inherent drive towards configuring disparate events into a narrative.[9] It endows significance to an event by making it a part of a sequence. Consequence is determined in sequence. Without the mutiny in Meerut, Mangal Pandey would have remained in obscurity like the sepoys of 1824–25, and without the fall of Delhi, the Meerut mutiny would have been an episode in a history of mutinies in India.

Any narrative needs a beginning. Thus, an event in Barrackpore on 29 March 1857 becomes a prelude to a sequence of events:

[9]See Hayden White, 'The Value of Narrative in the Representation of Reality' in his *The Content of the Form: Narrative Discourse and Historical Representation*.

it becomes a cardinal event, which directs the further course of events.[10] Mangal Pandey' s actions are thus made to configure in the narrative of a bigger event, the uprising of 1857. The uprising itself, by another shift in the narrative register by nationalist historians, is made part of an even bigger narrative, the history of India's freedom struggle. In this process of appropriation of an episode into narrative(s), Mangal Pandey is made a hero, a martyr, the first in a long roll call of honour.

[10]The ideas of cardinal event and the relationship between sequence and consequence are taken from Roland Barthes, 'Introduction to the Structural Analysis of Narratives' in his *Image, Music, Text.*

CHAPTER SEVEN

Appendix: Excerpts from documents on the trial of Mangal Pandey

The proceedings of the trial of Mangal Pandey are available in Forrest's *Selections* and have been extensively used in the main text of this book. But I thought it would be worthwhile to reprint the relevant parts of this record for a number of reasons. First, this is the only source that we have on the sepoy. All that one knows about him comes from these documents. Second, I thought that since my interpretation of Mangal Pandey's action runs somewhat against the grain of the prevalent historiographical opinion especially that of nationalist historiography, it would be best to make the principal documents available to readers so that they could form their own opinions and evaluate the validity or otherwise of my interpretation.

There is one other reason for reprinting these documents with this book. The proceedings of the trial were recorded and preserved as per the practice of the Company's administration. They are part of a huge archive of similar courts martial in the Bengal Army. What is important for this set is that they were recorded before the events of the revolt of 1857 engulfed the British and dismantled the elaborate administrative machinery that had been set up since the Company had acquired political power. In the summer of 1857, once the British counter-insurgency operations began in north India, such courts martial were abandoned. No legal procedures were followed and no records were kept. Through a series of Acts passed between May and June 1857, Britons were given the power to judge and take the lives of Indians without recourse to the due processes of law. An English civilian wrote in June, 'I have been appointed chief of a commission for the trial of all natives charged with offences against government and persons; day by day we have strung up eight and ten men. We have the power of life and death in our hands; and I assure we spare not. A very summary trial is all that takes place.' (See Mukherjee, *Spectre of Violence*, pp. 25–27)

The trial of Mangal Pandey was not, as these documents show, a summary one. Witnesses were called to testify, the accused was given the option to cross-examine and to speak for himself. The verdict of the court was arrived through a vote which was recorded. The process had certain lacunae to which we have drawn attention in the chapter on the trial, but it is important to underline that there was an established procedure which was followed in the case of Mangal Pandey. This suggests that British administration in March-April 1857 was very much in control. They saw in the defiance of Mangal Pandey an act of gross insubordination and mutiny but did not see it as a signal for a wider conflagration.

THE DOCUMENTS

Proceedings in continuation of a native General Court-martial assembled at Fort William, and re-assembled at Barrackpore on Monday, the 6th April 1857, by order of the Major-General Hearsey, for the trial of Sepoy Mungul Pandy, 34th Regiment, Native Infantry, and all prisoners who may be brought before it.

PRESIDENT:
Subadar-Major Howahir Lan Tewary, 43rd Regiment, Native Infantry.

MEMBERS:
Subadar Bhola Opudeah, 17th Regiment. Native Infantry.
Subadar Hurruck Sing, 40th Regiment, Native Infantry.
Subadar Ram Sing, 9th Battalion, Artillery.
Subadar Amanut Khan, 37th Regiment, Native Infantry.
Subadar Sewumbur Pandy, 34th Regiment, Native Infantry.
Subadar Dirga Ram, 70th Regiment, Native Infantry.
Subadar Khooda Buksh, 2nd Regiment. Native Infantry.
Subadar Meerwan Sing, 70th Regiment, Native Infantry.
Subadar Sookhlal Misr, 43rd Regiment. Native Infantry.

Subadar Ajoodhia Tewary, 70th Regiment, Native Infantry.
Subadar Jalim Sing, 43rd Regiment, Native Infantry.
Jamadar Dewan Allie, 9th Battalion, Artillery.
Jamadar Mohun Sing, 65th Regiment, Native Infantry.
Jamadar Lalla Ram Buksh, 8th Regiment, Native Infantry.

JUDGE ADVOCATE:
Captain G.C. Hatch, Deputy Judge Advocate-General, Presidency Division.

INTERPRETER:
Lieutenant James Vallings, 19th Regiment, Native Infantry.

The Court re-assembled at the Mess House of the 34th Regiment, Native Infantry, at Barrackpore, at 11 a.m., the President, Members, Judge Advocate, Interpreter all being present.

Lieutenant and Brevet-Colonel S.G. Wheler Commanding the 34th Regiment. Native Infantry, being appointed Prosecutor, takes his place in Court.

Mungal Pandy, Sepoy, No. 1446, 5th Company, 34th Regiment, Native Infantry, is brought a prisoner in Court.

The Division Orders directing the re-assembly of the Court-martial at Barrackpore, and the Station Order directing the hour and place of the Court's assembly, are produced and read.

The names of the President and Members of the Court are read over to the prisoner.

BY THE JUDGE ADVOCATE
Question: Sepoy Mungul Pandy, do you object to being tried by the president or by any of the Members of this Court-martial?
Answer: No, I do not object.

The interpreter, President, Members, and Judge Advocate make the prescribed solemn affirmation.

The following charge is read:

Mungul Pandy, Sepoy, No. 1446. 5th Company, 34th Regiment, Native Infantry, confined by order of Major-General J.B. Hearsey, Commanding the Presidency Division, on the following charges:

1st—For mutiny, in having at Barrackpore, on the 29th March 1857, gone on to the parade ground in front of the quarter-guard of his regiment armed with a sword and musket, and then and there used words tending to incite the men of his regiment to turn out and join him in resistance to lawful authority.

2nd—For having, on the occasion set forth in the first charge, used violence against his superior officers Sergeant-Major James Thornton Hewson and Lieutenant and Adjutant Bempde Henry Baugh, of the 34th Regiment, Native Infantry, by discharging at them, severally, his loaded musket, and then and there striking and wounding with his sword the said Lieutenant B.H. Baugh and Sergeant-Major J.T. Hewson.

By order of the Major-General Commanding Presidency Division.

ASST. ADJT. GENL.'S OFFICER (Sd.) A.H. ROSS, Major, BARRACKPORE; Asst. Adjt. Genl., Presy. Divn.
The 5th April 1857.

BY THE JUDGE ADVOCATE
Question: Sepoy Mungul Pandy, No. 1446, 5th Company, 24th Regiment, Native Infantry, how say you, are you guilty, or not guilty, of these charges?
Answer: Not guilty.
The handcuffs are removed from the prisoner.

PROSECUTION
First Witness Lieutenant and Brevet-Colonel S.O. Wheler, Commanding the 34th Regiment, Native Infantry, the Prosecutor, is sworn.

BY THE JUDGE ADVOCATE
Question: You commanded the 34th Regiment, Native Infantry?
Answer: Yes.
Question: On the 29th March last, did you go down to the quarter-guard of your regiment?
Answer: Yes.
Question: Why did you go?
Answer: Captain Drury drove up to my house in the afternoon of that day, informing me that a man, a sepoy, had gone out in front, inciting the men to mutiny. I proceeded with him to the parade—the lines I mean.

Question: What did you observe there?

Answer: I observed the sepoy in front, the prisoner walking parallel with a musket and sword. I proceeded in rear of the bell of arms to the quarter-guard. I did so, as several men about told me if I went in front of the bell-of-arms I should be shot. On arriving at the quarter-guard, it having been reported to me that the prisoner had wounded Lieutenant Baugh and the sergeant-major, I directed three or four men of the quarter-guard to load. They did load. I then directed the whole of the guard to load, and ordered the native office in command of the guard to seize the prisoner. He hesitated, and said that the men would not touch the prisoner. I repeated the order two or three times, when he gave the order to advance. The guard did so a few paces, and then halted, and he, the native officer, returned and said the men would not advance. As the Brigadier was on the parade. I went and reported the matter to him. To the best of my recollection, the General came up to the flank of the 34th Regiment, and after a few words with the Brigadier, he rode to the quarter-guard accompanied by several officers who were present at the time. The General directed the native officer to bring his guard in front. They advanced a few paces, when the prisoner shot himself.

Question: Where was the sepoy, Mungul Pandy, during these occurrences, and what was he doing?

Answer: He was walking up and down the parade parallel with the lines, about a hundred yards from the quarter-guard.

Question: Did you hear him say anything?

Answer: He spoke some thing; but I could not distinguish what he said.

Question: Did you observe the sergeant-major of the regiment and the adjutant?

Answer: No.

Question: Has there been of late anything unusual in the state of some of the sepoys of this station?

Answer: Towards the latter end of January there was much talking amongst the sepoys, I understood, generally, of the new cartridges being made up, and in consequence they had an idea that we were going to make them Christians by force.

Question: Were any and what measures adopted by the Major-General Commanding the Division, within your knowledge, to allay this feeling?

Answer: There was a general parade ordered on the 9th of February of the whole of the troops off duty at the station, when the General addressed them about the new cartridge paper.
Question: On the 29th March had any European troops arrived at this station?
Answer: A few were reported to be at the ghat, the Flag Staff Ghat, at this station.
Question: Were not the 19th Regiment, Native Infantry expected to arrive about that time in this station'?
Answer: Yes.
Question: Was it made known to the native troops at this station for what purpose that regiment was to be marched in?
Answer: At the general parade, on the 18th March, the General informed to the troops that the 19th Regiment, Native Infantry, would be disbanded on account of what took place at Berhampore.

The prisoner declined to cross-examine.

The Court now rose and proceeded to the bungalow of the sergeant-major, 43rd Regiment, Native Infantry, in order to take the evidence of Sergeant-Major J.T. Hewson, 34th Regiment, Native Infantry, reported not to be in a fit state to attend at the Court, the prisoner and all parties being present.

Second, Witness Sergeant-Major J.T. Hewson, 34th Regiment, Native Infantry, is duly sworn.

BY THE PROSECUTOR
Question: What are your Christian names?
Answer: James Thornton.
Question: Will you state the occurrences of the 29th of March last?
Answer: Between the hours of four and six on the 29th of March, the naick of the quarter-guard of the 34th Regiment. Native Infantry, Emam Khan, No. 5 Company, came to my bungalow and reported that Sepoy Mungul Pandy of No. 5 Company had armed himself with his musket loaded, and was walking about in front of the quarter-guard. He said that Mungul Pandy had taken a quantity of bhang, an intoxicating drug. I ordered the naick to report the circumstance to the adjutant of the regiment. I then went on the parade dressed in uniform, and with my sword. On arriving in front of the light company's bell of arms, a sepoy, regimentally dressed but with his dhotee on, no pantaloons, with

coat and belt, took deliberate aim and fired at me. The shot did not take effect. I then went in rear of the bells-of-arms towards the quarter-guard, and on my way there called out to the guard to fall in. On arriving at the quarter-guard, I found some of the men dressing and some dressed. I spoke to the native officer, Jemadar Issuree Pandy, in command of the quarter-guard; I asked him why he did not arrest the sepoy. He said: 'What can I do; my naick is gone to the adjutant; the havildar is gone to the field officer; am I to take him myself?' I ordered him to fall in his guard, and load. Some of the men grumbled; and he never insisted on the men loading or falling in. I then placed a sentry on the right and the left of the quarter-guard to watch Mungul Pandy. I saw Jemadar Gunness Lalla, No. 5 Company, and also Mookta Persad Pandy, colour-havildar of No. 5 Company, Jemadar Gunness Lalla spoke to Mungul Pandy the prisoner now before me. I could not understand all he said nor repeat it in Hindustani. What I heard Gunness Lalla, the jemadar, say was to give up his arms. A little after I heard the sound of horses' hoofs, and Lieutenant Baugh the Adjutant came riding up. The adjutant called out 'Where is he? Where is he?' I called out to him to look to his left, and then I said 'Sir, ride to the right for your life, the sepoy will fire at you.' I then saw Mungul Pandy, the prisoner, present his piece and fire. The adjutant's horse dropped. I saw him take aim. Lieutenant Baugh then dismounted and drew a pistol from his holster and fired at Mungul Pandy, the prisoner. The shot did not take effect from what I could see. The adjutant then drew his sword and rushed towards Mungal Pandy, the prisoner. When I saw him do so, I drew my sword and followed him, at the same time calling out to the guard to load and come on. I believe we both came up at the same time in front of the prisoner. Mungul Pandy made a cut with a *tulwar* (native sword) at me, but did not strike me. He struck the adjutant. The next cut I received myself from Mungul Pandy with his sword. At the same time I was knocked from behind by one or two blows from a sepoy's musket I could not recognize the features of the man who struck me; he was regimentally dressed. On rising up I advanced again towards the prisoner, and caught him by the collar of the coat with the left hand. I struck him several times with my sword, and received another cut from his *tulwar*. I was again knocked down from behind, and I remember being struck on the back and on the head when on the ground. The second time I was knocked down I was stupefied. On getting on my legs again. I saw a number of sepoys in front of the quarter-guard dressed. I also saw Lieutenant Baugh walking slowly towards the 43rd Regiment, Native Infantry, lines. His jacket had much blood on it. I followed him. On coming near my own bungalow, I heard footsteps behind me, and on turning round I saw Jemadar Issuree Pandy of the quarter-guard. I told him he had acted in a shameful manner, and that I would put him under arrest. I tried to grasp his sword, but he stepped back. His sword was in the scabbard. I then met my wife and step-daughter, who brought me to the bungalow of the sergeant-major of the 43rd. I there saw Lieutenant Baugh, and then saw *his* hand much cut.

Question: Did you hear Sepoy Mungul Pandy, the prisoner say anything when he was in front of the quarter-guard?

Answer: Yes. *'Nikul ao, pultan; rikul ao hamara sath'* 'Come out men; come out and join me. You sent me out here, why don't you' follow me.'

Question: When the sepoy fired at you, did you hear the sound of a bullet passing or striking anything?

Answer: I heard the sound of a bullet close.

Question: Was any effort whatever made *by* the jemadar in command of, or men of, the quarter-guard to come to your aid?

Answer: I had no assistance; the men who came struck me and Lieutenant Baugh once. I saw Lieutenant Baugh struck with a musket from behind.

Question: Did you hear any shot fired after you had gone out to the front with Lieutenant Baugh?

Answer: Yes, from the direction of the lines behind me, quite close. I think the shot passed between me and Lieutenant Baugh.

Question: At what distance did this affair occur from the quarter-guard?

Answer: About thirty or forty yards.

Question: How many men came up to where you and Lieutenant Baugh were?

Answer: When I left the place where I was struck down, there were seven or eight men. They were regimentally dressed, and I believe they belong to the quarter-guard.

Question: Why do you believe they belong to the quarter-guard?

Answer: When I left the quarter-guard to assist Lieutenant Baugh the quarter-guard was dressed, and the time was too short for other men to dress themselves and come out; and the men going on picket wear blue pantaloons; these men had white pantaloons on. There was one man I recognized—but I could not swear to him—Heeralall Tewary of that company, who struck me. He was on the quarter-guard.

Question: Did you see any men of the regiment assembled and looking on'?

Answer: Yes, there was a great number looking on from between the bell-of-arms, chiefly on the left, because three of the right wing companies have gone to Chittagong.

Question: Did any of these men come out to assist?

Answer: I did not see one. All the time I was out I kept my eye on the prisoner.

Question: Did you hear the jemadar of the quarter-guard or the men say anything when you were near them?

Answer: No, they were talking between themselves.

Question: How many sword cuts did you receive?

Answer: Two on the head.

Question: Are you now suffering from these wounds?

Answer: Yes.

(The witness is very much exhausted, and is lying on the *charpoy*.)

The prisoner declines to cross-examine.

The Court now, at 3 p.m. rose and proceeded to the quarters of Lieutenant B.H. Baugh, Adjutant, 34th Regiment, Native Infantry, reported unable to leave his quarters; the prisoner and all parties being present.

Third Witness Lieutenant B.H. Baugh, Adjutant, 34th Regiment, Native Infantry, is duly sworn.

BY THE PROSECUTOR

Question: You are Lieutenant Bempde Henry Baugh, and Adjutant, 34th Regiment, Native Infantry?

Answer: Yes.

Question: Will you be so good as to state the occurrences of the 29th March last?

Answer: On Sunday week last, at about five o'clock in the afternoon, the havildar-major of the regiment came to my quarters and reported that a sepoy of the name of Mungul Pandy, No. 5 Company, had turned out in front of the quarter-guard of the regiment and fired at the sergeant-major. I told the man to go and report the circumstance to Colonel Wheler, ordered my charger, put on my uniform, and after having put a brace of pistols in the holsters, I galloped down as hard as I could to the regimental quarter-guard. I had scarcely pulled up at the quarter when a shot was fired, and my horse fell under me. As soon as I could disentangle myself, I drew a pistol from the left holster, and on seeing the prisoner in the act of re-loading I fired. He stopped loading. I immediately drew my sword, and rushed in to secure him. I had proceeded about half way when the prisoner drew a tulwar. I looked back to see where my horse was, intending to get my other pistol, but saw that he was gone; so continued my advance and engaged the prisoner. After a conflict of about, perhaps, five or eight minutes (during which time I received a sword cut which entirely disabled my left hand, from the prisoner, also a very deep wound in my neck, and another on my head; the last, however, I am not certain whether it was a sword cut or proceeded from the butt end of a musket) a shot was fired close by: it came from the direction of the quarter-guard. On finding myself gradually getting hemmed in, I commenced retreating. During this time, with the exception of Shaik Pultoo, sepoy, Grenadier Company, not a man either from the regimental quarter-guard or from the lines advanced to my assistance. Shaik Pultoo held the prisoner, and enabled me to make my retreat good. I reached the sergeant-major's bungalow of the 43rd Regiment, Native (Light) Infantry, and from there was conveyed by Captain Wiggins to Dr. Allen's, to have my wounds dressed.

Question: How far from the quarter-guard of the regiment did this take place?

Answer: My horse was shot at about, I should say, eight or nine paces from the quarter-guard of the regiment; and the conflict took place, I should say, about forty or fifty paces.

Question: Did you receive the wound in your neck also from the prisoner?

Answer: Yes.

Question: When you rode up, were many men standing in front and about the lines?

Answer: A great number.

Question: Did you observe whether any of the men who came up to you during the conflict were regimentally dressed?
Answer: I could not observe; I was so busily engaged in warding off the prisoner's blows.
Question: Did the prisoner say anything when you were fighting with *him?*
Answer: Not that I recollect.
Question: Was your horse wounded with a bullet?
Answer: Yes.
Question: When your attention was first directed to the prisoner, where did you see him?
Answer: He was to my left about fifty yards from me, in front of the quarter-guard.

The prisoner declines to cross-examine.

The Court returns to their first place of assembly, the 34th Regiment Mess House, the Court, prisoner, and Prosecutor all being present.

Fourth Witness Drummer John Lewis, 34th Regiment, Native Infantry, is called into Court and duly affirmed.

BY THE PROSECUTOR
Question: Were you on duty as bugler at the quarter-guard of your regiment at Barrackpore on Sunday the 29th March last?
Answer: I was drummer of the guard.
Question: State what you saw in the afternoon.
Answer: After four o'clock in the afternoon, the prisoner came towards the quarter-guard, crying out, where is the bugler. Upon seeing me, he told me to sound the assembly. I did not obey through fear. He then pointed his musket at me. I did not then obey; on seeing a sepoy near, he said to him, lowering his musket towards him, 'Why are you not getting ready? It is for our religion.' He remained there for sometime repeating the words 'sound the assembly'. When the sergeant-major arrived after some time. I saw from my place where I had sheltered myself that he fired his musket at the sergeant-major, who was advancing from the left wing. I did not know where the ball struck. I heard the sound of the ball. About a quarter of an hour afterwards the adjutant also arrived from the direction of the left wing. I saw

the prisoner fire his musket at the adjutant and hit the horse. The horse dropped, and the adjutant, disengaging himself, went towards prisoner on foot, with a pistol in his hand. The sergeant major went also with him. The prisoner again fired his musket. I saw the prisoner also strike the sergeant-major and the adjutant with a sword.

Question: What did the jemadar of the guard do all this time?
Answer: The jemadar went towards the rear-guard.
Question: When the conflict was going on between the adjutant and sepoy, where was the jemadar of the quarter-guard?
Answer: He was present in the guard.

The witness appearing to be alarmed, is told not to be frightened.
Question: What did the jemadar of the guard do while the fight was going on?
Answer: He was standing amongst his guard. He did nothing.
Question: Did you go up with the guard to the place where the fight was going on?
Answer: I did not go.
Question: Did any of the guard go?
Answer: I did not see anyone go.
Question: Did sepoy Heeralall Tewary go or not?
Answer: I don't know him.
Question: Did the jemadar and men of the guard go to where the fight was going on?
Answer. No: He did not go with the guard.

The prisoner declines to cross-examine.
(The questioning of Drummer John Lewis continues)

BY THE COURT
Question: When Mungul Pandy, Sepoy, came first to the guard, how near did he come up?
Answer: About some thirteen paces.
Question: Where was the jemadar then?
Answer: I was sewing, and did not see him.
Question: Do you know where he was?
Answer: He was inside the quarter-guard.
Question: Did any one of the quarter-guard attempt to secure the prisoner?
Answer: No one attempted.

Question: Did the jemadar give any orders to secure the prisoner?
Answer: No, not any.

Fifth Witness Havildar Shaik Pultoo, 34th Regiment. Native Infantry, is called into court and duly affirmed.

BY THE PROSECUTOR
Question: On the 29th of March you were a sepoy in the Grenadier Company were you not and are now promoted to havildar?
Answer. Yes; I am now havildar.
Question: Relate what you saw on the parade on the afternoon of the 29th March last.
Answer: About half-past three I had gone out to ease myself; and on returning to the lines, I observed Mungul Pandy in his coat and hat; and accoutrements and musket in his hand. He was shouting out. 'Come out, you bhainchutes, the Europeans are here. From biting these cartridges, we shall become infidels. Get ready, turn out all of you.' He came out of his hut—I saw him—and ordered the bugler to sound the assembly. The two drummers hid themselves. The sergeant-major came up, and the sepoy then fired at him. The sergeant-major said to the jemadar of the quarter-guard, 'See you have done nothing, and he has shot at me.' Mungul Pandy was walking up and down in front of the quarter-guard, about thirty paces off.
Question: Did you see the adjutant come up?
Answer: No.
Question: What happened then?
Answer: The adjutant came up and looked round him, and then the sepoy, Mungul Pandy, shot the horse in the left thigh.
Question: Did he take aim'?
Answer: Yes.
Question: What happened then?
Answer: The horse fell. The adjutant then took a pistol out of one holster and said to me, 'Shaik Pultoo, no one is assisting me, you come with me.' We then advanced and the sergeant-major also. On reaching the sepoy, he struck the adjutant with his sword and wounded him in the hand, and afterwards the sergeant-major also on the head. The sepoy struck them again. I came up and caught him by the waist. He wounded me in the hand. The sepoys in uniform struck the adjutant and sergeant-major also, who fell down, with the butts of their muskets.

Question: What sepoys were there?
Answer: Sepoys of the quarter-guard; they were in uniform.
Question: Do you know them?
Answer: No I was twenty paces off. The adjutant was retreating when they strock him.
Question: How many sepoys were there in uniform?
Answer: I saw four.
Question: Did you hear any shot fired while the adjutant and sepoy were fighting?
Answer: Yes; from the direction of the guard. The ball passed the Sergeant-Major and adjutant.
Question: Did you see where it was fired from?
Answer: It came from behind me and from the direction of the quarter-guard.
Question: Was sepoy Mungul Pandy in an excited state?
Answer: He eats bhang; I don't know if he had eaten any then.
Question: When the adjutant and sergeant-major retreated, what became of the sepoy, Mungul Pandy?
Answer: I had hold of him. I held him until the adjutant had gone off the ground. I called out to the jemadar of the guard, who was about thirty paces off, to send four sepoys to take charge of him.
Question: Did the jemadar send the sepoys to take charge of him?
Answer: No, not one.
Question: Did the jemadar give you any answer?
Answer: No, he was inside the quarter-guard.
Question: When did you release the sepoy?
Answer: When I could hold no longer. I was wounded.
Question: Did any sepoys interfere to make you let the man go?
Answer: Yes.
Question: Who were they?
Answer: Some of the quarter-guard.
Question: Name them?
Answer: I don't know them. There was a crowd; they called out to me from inside the guard to let him go.

The witness withdraws.

The prosecution is closed.

The prisoner being called on for his defence says, 'I did not know who I wounded and who I did not; what more shall I say? I have nothing more to say.'

The prisoner being asked, says, 'I have no evidence.'

Question: Have you anything to disclose, or do you wish to say anything?
Answer: No.
Question: Did you act on Sunday last by your own free will, or were you instructed by others?
Answer: Of my own will. I expected to die.
Question: Did you load your own musket to save your life?
Answer: No, I intended to take it.
Question: Did you intend to take the adjutant's life, or would you have shot anyone else?
Answer: I should have shot anyone who came.
Question: Were you under the influence of any drugs?
Answer: Yes, I have been taking bhang and opium of late, but formerly never touched any drugs. I was not aware at the, time of what I was doing.

The prisoner was asked frequently if he would give up the names of any connected with the occurrence, and was given to understand that he had nothing to fear from his own regiment by disclosing anything, but he refused to state more than the above.

The sepoy attending him was removed from the tent during the investigation.

The defence is closed.

The Court is closed.

FINDING

The Court find the prisoner Mungul Pandy, Sepoy, No. 1446, 5th Company, 34th Regiment, Native Infantry, guilty of both charges preferred against him.

The Court is re-opened, and the prisoner brought before it.

Captain C.C. Drury, 34th Regiment, Native Infantry is called and sworn.

BY THE JUDGE ADVOCATE

Question: Has the prisoner been warned that his former convictions and general character will be brought in evidence against him?

Answer: There were no previous convictions; he has been warned as to his general character.

Question: What is the prisoner's general character?

Answer: Good.

Question: What is his age and length of service'?

Answer: His age is twenty-six years, two months and nine days. His service is seven years, two months and nine days.

The Prisoner declines to cross-examine.
The Court is closed.

SENTENCE

The Court sentenced the prisoner, Mungul Pandy, Sepoy, No. 1446, 5th Company, 34th Regiment, Native Infantry, to suffer death by being hanged by the neck until he be dead.

Approved and confirmed.
BARRACKPORE (Sd.) J.B. HEARSEY, Maj. Genl.

The 7th April 1857, Comdg. The Presy. Divn.

From Captain G.C. Hatch, Deputy Judge Advocate-General, to Major-General J.B. Hearsey, C.B., Commanding the Presidency Division, dated Barrackpore, 6 April 1857.

I have the honour to make the following reports to you in regard to the state of the votes of the officers forming the general court martial on the trial of Sepoy Mungul Pandy, 34th Regiment, Native Infantry;

1st—That the verdict was carried by the votes of fourteen officers on the first charge; and by the votes of fourteen officers on the second charge.

2nd—That eleven officers voted for the sentence of death.

The execution of Mungul Pandy, Sepoy, No. 1446, 5th Company, 34th Regiment, Native Infantry, will take place on the, bridge parade tomorrow morning, the 8th instant, at half-past five o'clock in presence of all the troops off duty at the station. The Court adjourned at 6.30 p.m.

Bibliography

Alavi, Seema, The *Sepoys and the Company: Tradition and Transition in Northern India, 1770–1830* (Delhi, 1995).

Ball, C., *The History of the Indian Mutiny*, 2 vols (London, nd).

Bandyopadhyay, P.K., *Tulsi Leaves and the Ganges Water:* The *Slogan of the First Sepoy Mutiny in Barrackpore* (Kolkata, 2003).

Barat, A., *The Bengal Native Infantry: Its Organization and Discipline, 1796–1852* (Calcutta, 1962).

Barthes, Roland, *Image, Music;. Text* (London, 1984).

Butter, D., *Outline of the Topography and Statistics of the Southern Districts of Oudh* (Calcutta, 1839).

Chaudhuri, S.B., *Civil Rebellion in the Indian Mutinies (1857–59)* (Calcutta, 1957).

______, *English Historical Writings on the Indian Mutiny (1857–59)* (Calcutta. 1979).

Coopland, R.M., *A Lady's Escape from Gwalior* (London, 1859).

David. Saul, *The Indian Mutiny: 1857* (London, 2002).

Edwardes, H.B. and Merivale, H., *Life of Sir Henry Lawrence*, 2 vols (London, 1873).

Forrest, G.W., *Selections from the Letters. Despatches and Other State Papers Preserved in the Military Department of the Government of India, 1857–58*, 4 vols (Calcutta, 1893–1912).

Gubbins, M., *An Account of the Mutinies in Oude and the Siege of the Lucknow Residency* (London, 1858).

Guha. Ranajit, *Elementary Aspects of Peasant Insurgency in Colonial India* (Delhi, 1983).

______,The Prose of Counter Insurgency' in Ranajit Guha (ed.), *Subaltern Studies: Writings on South Asian History and Society*, vol. 2 (Delhi, 1983).

______, *Dominance Without Hegemony: History and Power in Colonial India* (Delhi, 1998).
Gupta, P.C., *Nana Sahib and the Rising at Cawnpore* (Oxford, 1963).
Hibbert, C., *The Great Mutiny: India, 1857* (Harmondsworth, 1978).
Kaye, J.W., *History of the Sepoy War, 1857–58*, 3 vols (London, 1864–1880).
Majumdar. R.C., The *Sepoy Mutiny and the Revolt of 1857* (Calcutta, 1957).
Maude, F.C., *Memories of the Mutiny*, 2 vols (London, 1894).
Mukherjee, R., *Awadh in Revolt*, 1857–58: *A Study of Popular Resistance* (Delhi, 1984, repr., 2002).
______, *Spectre of Violence: The 1857 Kanpur Massacres* (Delhi, 1998).
Palmer, J.A.B., *The Mutiny Outbreak at Meerut in 1857* (Cambridge, 1966).
Ray, Tapti, *The Politics of a Popular Uprising: Bundelkhand* in 1857 (Delhi, 1996).
Reeves, Peter (ed.), *Sleeman in Oudh* (Cambridge, 1971).
Rizvi, S.A., and Bhargava, M.L. (eds), *Freedom Struggle in Uttar Pradesh*, 6 vols (Lucknow, 1957).
Russell, W.R., *My Indian Mutiny Diary* (ed. M. Edwardes), (London, 1957).
Savarkar, V.D., *The Indian War of Independence, 1857* (London, 1909).
Sen, S.N., *1857* (Delhi, 1957).
Sinha, Kaliprasanna, *Hootum Pyanchar Naksha* (Calcutta, 1862).
Sitaram, *From Sepoy to Subedar* (ed. James Lunt, tr. Capt. Norgate) (London, 1970).
Sleeman, W.H., *A Journey through the Kingdom of Oude in 1849–50*, 2 vols (London, 1858).
Sripantha (Nikhil Sarkar), *Mangal Pandeyer Bichar* (Kolkata, 2004).
Stokes, Eric, *The Peasant and the Raj: Studies in Agrarian Society and Peasant Rebellion in Colonial India* (Cambridge, 1978).
______, *The Peasant Armed: The Indian Rebellion of 1857* (Bombay, 1986 (Oxford, 1986)).
Taylor, P.J.O., *Companion to the Indian Mutiny of 1857* (Delhi, 1996).
White, Hayden, *The Content of the Form: Narrative Discourse and Historical Representation* (Baltimore, 1987).

Index